WITH THE FIRE ON HIGH

WITH THE FIRE ON HIGH

ELIZABETH ACEVEDO

THORNDIKE PRESS
A part of Gale, a Cengage Company

Copyright © 2019 by Elizabeth Acevedo.
Thorndike Press, a part of Gale, a Cengage Company.

ALL RIGHTS RESERVED
Thorndike Press® Large Print Young Adult.
The text of this Large Print edition is unabridged.
Other aspects of the book may vary from the original edition.
Set in 16 pt. Plantin.

LIBRARY OF CONGRESS CIP DATA ON FILE.
CATALOGUING IN PUBLICATION FOR THIS BOOK
IS AVAILABLE FROM THE LIBRARY OF CONGRESS

ISBN-13: 978-1-4328-7184-0 (hardcover alk. paper)

Published in 2019 by arrangement with HarperCollins Children's Books,
a division of HarperCollins Publishers

Printed in Mexico
1 2 3 4 5 6 7 23 22 21 20 19

For the women in my family,
who have gathered me when I needed
gathering and given me a launchpad
when I needed to dream.

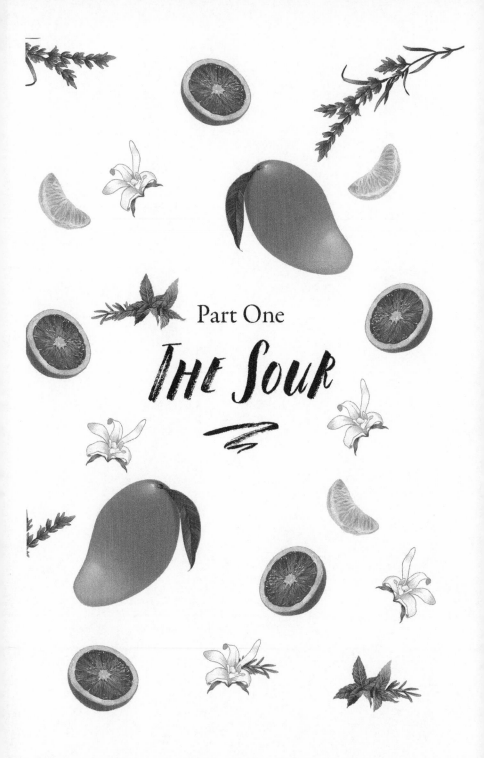

Part One

THE SOUR

Emoni's Recipe
"WHEN LIFE GIVES YOU LEMONS, MAKE LEMON VERBENA TEMBLEQUE"

Serves: Your heart when you are missing someone you love.

Ingredients:

Two cans of coconut milk
Handful of white sugar
Four shakes of cornstarch
Pinch of salt
Bunch of lemon verbena leaves
Bunch of vanilla beans
Cinnamon, enough to garnish

Directions:

1. In a saucepan, heat coconut milk until it comes to a boil. Muddle a bunch of lemon verbena leaves and vanilla beans and add to the heated

coconut milk. Let steep.

2. After fifteen minutes, mix the in-fused coconut milk, salt, sugar, and cornstarch. Stir the mixture until the cornstarch is completely dis-solved. Let the combined ingredi-ents come to a boil and keep stir-ring until the mixture begins getting pudding thick.

3. Pour into a big cereal bowl and cover with plastic wrap. Place in the refrigerator for five hours.

4. After removing the mixture from the cereal bowl mold, sprinkle with cinnamon.

*Best eaten cold while daydreaming about palm trees and listening to an Héc-tor Lavoe classic.

Day One

Babygirl doesn't even cry when I suck my teeth and undo her braid for the fourth time. If anything, I'm the one on the verge of tears, since at this rate we're both going to be late.

"Babygirl, I'm sorry. I know it hurts. Mommy just doesn't want you looking a hot mess."

She seems unfazed by my apology, probably because thing (1) I'm not braiding tight enough to actually hurt her (which is why her hair is all loosey-lopsided!), and thing (2) Babygirl is watching *Moana*. And she loves *Moana*. So long as I let her watch *Moana* she'll let me play with her hair till kingdom come. Thank goodness Angelica lets me use her Netflix account. I lean a little closer to the edge of the sofa so I can snatch up the baby hairs at the front of her head. This is the hardest part, and I have to start the braid tight and small to get it right.

"Emoni, vete. It's time for you to head out. I'll fix her hair."

I don't even look over at 'Buela standing by the staircase that leads to the two bedrooms upstairs. "I got it, 'Buela. I'm almost done."

"You're going to be late for school."

"I know, but . . ." I trail off and it turns out I don't have to say it, because in her way 'Buela always understands.

She walks over and picks up the comb from where I set it on the couch. "You wish you could be the one taking her."

I nod and bite my bottom lip. I worked so hard to get Babygirl into a good day-care, and despite a long wait list I kept calling and stopping by Mamá Clara's, the woman who runs the childcare, until she snuck us into an opening. Now that Babygirl is actually going I'm freaking out. In her entire two years on earth,

Babygirl has never not been with family. I braid to the very tip of her hair. The design is simple, some straight backs with a pink hair tie at the end that matches Babygirl's outfit: little white collared shirt and pink pullover. She looks adorable. I wasn't able to buy her more than three new outfits for daycare, but I'm glad I splurged on this one.

I pull Babygirl's chair around so we are face-to-face, but I catch her trying to sneak a peek at *Moana* from the corner of her eye. Even though my chest is tight, I giggle. Babygirl might still be young, but she's also learning to be real slick.

"Babygirl, Mommy needs to go to school. You make sure you're nice to the other kids and that you pay attention to Mamá Clara so you learn a lot, okay?" Babygirl nods as if I just gave her the most serious Jada Pinkett Smith success speech. I hug her to my stomach, making sure not to nuzzle her too tight and fuzz up the braids I spent an hour doing. With a final kiss on her forehead, I take a deep breath and grab my book bag off the sofa, making sure to wipe down the plastic cover so 'Buela doesn't get annoyed with me.

" 'Buela, don't forget her snacks. Mamá Clara said we need to supply them every day. Oh, and her juice! You know she gets fussy." As I walk past 'Buela, I lean in real hush-hush. "And I also packed a little bottle of water. I know she doesn't like it as much, but I don't want her only drinking sugary stuff, you know?"

'Buela looks like she's trying to swallow a smile as she puts a soft hand on my back and guides me toward the front door.

"Look at you trying to give me lessons on parenting. Nena, please! Like I didn't raise you! And your father." 'Buela gives my back a squeeze, smooths the hair bunned up high on my head. "She's going to be fine, Emoni. You make sure that *you* have a good first day of school. Be nice to the other kids. Learn a lot."

I lean against her for a quick second and inhale her signature vanilla scent. "Bendición, 'Buela."

"Que Dios te bendiga, nena." She swats me on the booty and opens the front door. The sounds of West Allegheny Avenue rush in to greet me: cars honking, buses screeching to a stop, rapid Spanglish yelled from the corners as people greet one another, and mothers calling out last-minute instructions to their kids from open windows. The door closes behind me and for a second my breath catches in sync with the lock. Every simple love in my life is behind this one wooden door. I press my ear against it and hear a clap of hands, then 'Buela says in a high, cheery voice, "Okay, Baby Emma! Today you're going to be a big girl!"

I pull the straps of my backpack tighter. Give myself that same pep talk as I race down the stairs: Okay, Emoni. Today? Time to be a big girl.

EMMA

I wanted to give Babygirl a nice name. The kind of name that doesn't tell you too much before you meet her, the way mine does. Because nobody ever met a white girl named Emoni, and as soon as they see my name on a résumé or college application they think they know exactly what kind of girl they getting. They know way more about me than they need to know, and shit — I mean, *shoot* — information ain't free, so my daughter's name isn't going to tell anybody any information they didn't earn. That's why I fought Tyrone tooth and nail to name her Emma.

"You just want her name to have the same letters as yours." Tyrone is a whiner.

"No. I want her name to sound less like either of ours," I said, and I don't remember if I kissed Babygirl's infant cheek or not. But I know in that moment I felt this huge emotion; I wanted to do whatever I could to give my daughter the best opportunity in the world. And although our names do have similar letters, mine is full of silverware-sharp sounds: *E-Mah-Nee.* Hers is soft, rolls off the tongue like a half-dreamed murmur.

Anyhow, Tyrone was late on the day I filled out the birth certificate, so Emma it was. I know a name alone can't guarantee new opportunities, but at the very least it'll give her a chance to get in the room, to let other people realize she's someone they want to learn more about.

SISTER FRIENDS

Angelica waits on the corner for me the way she has since elementary school. Her long dark hair has streaks the same bright red as her lipstick. She shuffles from foot to foot in the tightest leggings I have ever seen on a body.

I stop halfway to her and pretend to do a double take. "Girl, you about to give these boys a show! And it's only the first day," I say as she swoops her arm through mine and we walk in the direction of the bus stop.

"Girl, you know I ain't concerned with those boys. The ladies, on the other hand? I was social-media creeping and the summer did wonders for a lot of these jawns!"

I laugh and shake my head. "Does Laura know what she's gotten herself into?"

Angelica smiles and for a second she looks like the angel she's named after. "Aww, my boo knows I only look and don't touch. I just want her to know I can leave if I want to. I got options!"

Angelica officially came out last year and once she'd dusted the closet lint off her Air Maxes, she never looked back. A couple of months after coming out at home and at school, she met Laura at a graphic design workshop held for teens at the Philadelphia Museum of Art. Her girl Laura is built like the Vikings she says she's descended from: tall, thick-shouldered, and with an artist's gentle hands that I knew would take care of my best friend's heart.

"Man, whatever. I see all your posts about Laura. If you and that girl take another cutesy kissy picture, I'm going to delete my account. Actually, I'm going to hack in and delete yours!"

"Don't hate, Emoni. Is Tyrone still being a dick?"

I swat her on the arm. "This is why I don't let you around Babygirl; you have such a potty mouth."

"And you don't?" She gives me one of her pursed-lips looks.

"Yes, but I picked it up from *you*. And I've been working on it." I accidentally slipped in front of Babygirl a few weeks ago and almost died when I heard her saying "sh-sh-sh" as if practicing the word. I've cut out my cursing since.

"How is my niece? I haven't seen her since . . . when? Saturday?" We laugh. Despite her potty mouth, Angelica is great with Babygirl and always comes in clutch when either 'Buela or I can't watch her. Now that Babygirl's two, 'Buela insists that I have to take on more responsibility in raising her. Which I don't mind, since Babygirl is the coolest kid on the block. It's just hard juggling work, her, and now the new school year, without 'Buela taking on the big role she took the first two years of her life. And although I don't say it, I don't have to; Tyrone *is* still being a dick — an ass — *a prick*. Who uses the word *prick*?

"Hello! Emoni, are you listening?" Angelica snaps her fingers in my face.

"Sorry . . . I spaced out for a second. What'd you say?"

Angelica sighs dramatically. Anytime Angelica sighs, it's dramatically. "You never listen to me anymore."

I unhook my arm from hers. "Get out of here with that mess. All I do is listen to you."

"I was asking about the dinner you left for me and Babygirl when I babysat. What'd you call it?"

"Pollo guisado — stewed chicken. Was it good?" Angelica's been eating at my house since we were little girls, but since I always tweak what I cook, it's never the same thing twice. "I thought I might have messed up when I added in the collards at the end. They weren't in the original recipe."

"It was *so* good. I was wondering if you could make it for Laura and me. Six-month anniversary coming up in a month! I was thinking we could do a romantic dinner at my house since my moms is going to be out of town."

21

"Dinner at home is never romantic, Gelly," I say. The bus pulls up and we climb on with the rest of the people who, like us, are going to school and work near Yorktown and Fairmount and even farther south into Center City.

"Dinner at home will be romantic if it's catered by you!" We find a place to stand and hold on to the straps above us as the bus begins the jerky ten-minute ride.

"Now I'm a caterer? You're lucky I love you."

"No. I'm lucky you love to cook, and you never turn down an opportunity to practice on your friends. Chef Emoni Santiago, next *Chopped* champion!"

I laugh and pull my phone out to take notes for Gelly's dinner.

MAGIC

If you ask her to tell it, 'Buela starts with the same story.

I was a little older than Babygirl is now and always following 'Buela into the kitchen. I would sit at the kitchen table eating bootleg Cheerios or rice or something I could pick up with my fingers and shove into my mouth while she played El Gran Combo or Celia Cruz or La Lupe loud on her old-school radio, shimmying her hips while stirring a pot. She can't remember what made that day different — if my pops, Julio, had been late in arriving on one of his yearly visits from San Juan, or if it'd been a time she'd gotten reprimanded at work for taking too long on someone's measurements — but this particular day she didn't turn the radio on and she wasn't her usual self at the stove. At one point, she must have forgotten I was there because she threw the kitchen rag down on the floor and left. She just walked straight out of the kitchen, crossed the living room, opened the front door, and was gone.

We can't agree on what it was she'd started cooking. She says it was a stew and nothing that would burn quick, but although my own memory is childhood-fuzzy, I remember it being a pot of moro — the rice and beans definitely something that would soak up water. 'Buela says she just stepped out onto the stoop to clear her head, and when she came back ten minutes later I had pulled the step stool to the stove, had a bunch of spices on the counter, and had my small arm halfway into the pot, stirring.

It goes without saying: She. Had A. Fit. Thought I had been about to burn myself, dinner, or worse, the house. ('Buela would argue that's not the right order of things, and I know she would have definitely been upset if I hurt myself, but if I burned the house? Girl, there's no coming back from that.) All that to say, nothing charred. In fact, when 'Buela tasted it (whatever "it" was) she says it was the best thing she'd ever eaten. How it made her whole day better, sweeter. Says a memory of Puerto Rico she hadn't thought about in years reached out like an island hammock and cradled her close. When she tells the story, it's always a different simile, but still sweet like that. All I know is she cried into her plate that night. And so at the age of four, I learned someone could cry from a happy memory.

Ever since then 'Buela is convinced I have magical hands when it comes to cooking. And I don't know if I really have something special, or if her telling me I got something special has brainwashed me into believing it, but I do know I'm happier in the kitchen than anywhere else in the world. It's the one place I let go and only need to focus on the basics: taste, smell, texture, fusion, beauty.

And something special *does* happen when I'm cooking. It's like I can imagine a dish in my head and I just know that if I tweak this or mess with that, if I give it my special brand of sazón, I'll have made a dish that never existed before. Angelica thinks it's because we live in the hood, so we never have exactly the right ingredients — we gotta innovate, baby. My aunt Sarah says it's in our blood, an innate need to tell a story through food. 'Buela says it's definitely a blessing, magic. That my food doesn't just taste good, it *is* good — straight up bottled goodness that warms you and makes you feel better about your life. I think I just know that this herb with that veggie with that meat plus a dash of eso ahí will work.

And that if everything else goes wrong, a little squeeze of lime and a bottle of hot sauce ain't never hurt nobody.

THE AUTHORS

"All right, girlie, see you at lunch?" Angelica says as we stop outside my advisory. Advisory is Schomburg's fancy name for homeroom.

"Yeah, save me a seat by the windows if you get there first. Oh, and grab me —"

"Some applesauce if they look like they're running out. I know, Emoni." Angelica smirks and walks away. And she does know me. I *love* the school applesauce — extra cinnamony.

Ms. Fuentes has been my advisor since my first day at Schomburg Charter, and her classroom has never changed. Lady still has the same motivational sign above her door: *You're the Author of Your Own Life Story.* That sign has stared at us twenty advisory students from the time when we walked in as little-bitty fresh-men. And even though it doesn't make me roll my eyes anymore, I still think it's corny. Nonetheless, Advisory is my favor-ite class period of the day, even though it's also the shortest; it's where Ms. Fuentes takes attendance, makes an-nouncements, and gives us college prep and "character-building" exercises. But most important, it's the only class that has had the same students in it since freshman year. So we can talk here the way we can't in any other class.

Ms. Fuentes looks up from the class-room window shades to see me staring at her inspirational sign. "Ms. Santiago, how was your summer?" she says as she adjusts the shades so they let in more light. She does that, the Mr. This and Ms. That. Has since we walked into her classroom at fourteen. I sit at my desk in the second row, closest to the door. It was clutch when I was pregnant and had to rush to the bathroom every five minutes, and I haven't switched seats since.

I shrug. "Good. Got a job. Yours?"

Ms. Fuentes stops mid-shade-fussing to side-eye me. "You're always so loquacious. It's refreshing to have a student who believes in something other than monosyllables." But she's smiling. She's never said it, but I know I'm one of her favorites. Other students begin trickling into the room.

I smile back at her. "Aw, Ms. Fuentes, I see you worked on your sarcasm this summer. It's gotten so much better."

She stops messing with the windows and walks closer to my desk. She says softly, "How's Emma? Where'd you get a job?"

"She's real good, Ms. Fuentes. And the job is at the Burger Joint." Which, although it's spelled all official, I still pronounce "jawn." They think just because the Temple area has changed some that they gotta be fancy, but a burger jawn is a burger jawn regardless of how you spell it. "You know the spot near the university? I work there after school two days during the week and four hours every weekend."

Her pretty, manicured nails tap on my desk and I imagine she's tracing her finger along a mental map of North Philly.

"Yes, I think I've passed it before. Are you going to be able to juggle everything while also working there?"

I drop my eyes to my desk. "I should be okay. It's not that many hours."

"I see. . . . I know senior year is already stressful; try not to take on too much."

And I don't know what to say. It's *not* that many hours; in fact, I wish it were more. The cash I get from those little checks helps with groceries, Babygirl's expenses, and whatever 'Buela's disability money doesn't cover.

My silence doesn't faze Ms. Fuentes at all. "I have a surprise for you when the bell rings — a class I think you would love."

She squeezes my shoulder before giving her attention to Amir Robinson from the Strawberry Mansion area. "Welcome back, Mr. Robinson! Jesus, but you grew over the summer!" Ms. Fuentes walks away, calling out, "Ms. Connor, I dusted off your favorite seat in the back row just for you. . . ."

THAT GIRL

Yup. I was *that* girl your moms warns you about being friends with. And warns you about becoming. Not even done with freshman year of high school and already a belly that extended past my toes. It's a good thing Babygirl was born in August since I probably would have failed out if I had to go to school the last month of my pregnancy. And the thing with being pregnant as a teen is that your body isn't the only thing that changes. It wasn't just that I always had to pee, or that my back always hurt. It wasn't only that my feet ached and I cooked the *funkiest* meals (they were still so good they'd make you twerk something, but definitely off the wall: macaroni jalapeño burgers and Caribbean jerk lamb tacos).

The biggest changes weren't the ones that happened to my body at all.

It was that 'Buela had to scrounge up more sewing jobs to supplement the money she gets from disability, that the viejos playing dominoes on the corner shook their heads when I walked past, that dudes on the train smirked at my swollen boobs but wouldn't give up their seats; that I had to take a million make-up tests for the days I was at doctor appointments or too morning-sick to make it to school.

When they first learned I was pregnant, Principal Holderness and the guidance counselor called a special meeting in the main office. 'Buela had to come into school and they called in Ms. Fuentes, too. Principal Holderness and the counselor offered to transfer me to an alternative high school program specifically for pregnant teens. But Ms. Fuentes didn't play that. She said switching me midyear into a new school would be a hard adjustment, and that since the program had a decelerated curriculum it would affect my graduating on time. I know she called 'Buela beforehand to discuss it, and they must have come up with a plan, because 'Buela was quick to chime in, saying my staying at Schomburg Charter would be "pivotal for my retention and matriculation." The sentence sounded as if she'd rehearsed it, circling her mouth over those words in the mirror to make sure she got it right, and I know it was Ms. Fuentes who had explained to 'Buela what that meeting would be about. I didn't even know what those words meant at the time, but I know now Ms. Fuentes was fighting to help keep me a regular kid for as long as possible.

I've always been small: physically petite, which made people think I had a small personality, too. And then, all of a sudden, I was a walking PSA: a bloated teen warning, taking up too much space and calling too much attention.

IMMERSED

"I've got two announcements," Ms. Fuentes says.

"Ms. Fuentes," Amir calls out without raising his hand. "You better not say you leaving."

"No, no. Nothing like that, Mr. Robinson," she says, and we all slump a bit in relief. "The first announcement is that there are going to be changes to the schedule. In August some new faculty members were hired, and needless to say, it has affected class schedules. There are new elective courses being offered for seniors, and I'm going to pass around the new course listing. The second announcement is about a new student."

We all groan. In almost every class I've

ever had, students come and go throughout the entire year and nobody cares. But
Advisory is different. Nobody wants to
talk around no strangers that aren't going to last long.

"I know, I know. I've fought the administration tooth and nail to keep Advisory
small and with the same students, but
there just isn't room anywhere else. I've
met the student and I think he'll be a
great fit. He's registering today, but when
he comes in tomorrow make sure you're
all on your best behavior. I just wanted
to give you a heads-up. Now, let's talk
about electives."

Ms. Fuentes smiles and slides a hand-
out onto each of our desks.

"Look carefully at this list, think about
what class is the best fit, and get back to
me tomorrow."

We all pick up our bags at the ringing
bell. I wave to Ms. Fuentes on my way
out, looking at the long list of electives.
The old favorites are still there: Photog-
raphy, Creative Writing, Woodshop,
Dance. And there, tucked at the bottom
of the list:

Culinary Arts: Spain Immersion.

The class title balloons and rises above the rest, growing in my vision until I can't make out the other words. In all my time at Schomburg Charter there has never been a culinary arts elective — even though the school has both a classroom kitchen and an unused café from years past. I imagine this class is going to fill right up.

And for a second, excitement bubbles inside me like a simmering pot. I can finally take an official cooking class, and one with a specific regional focus. And then I remember, it's senior year. The responsible thing to do would be to stay with my current schedule and keep my study hall. Not add another class or more work. I turn down the simmer of excitement until it dies.

Two periods later, I meet Angelica at the cafeteria entrance and she eyes the line as if she's trying to find someone who will let us cut. "Did you see the graphic design elective? You should take it with me!"

I shake my head. Girl knows I'm not doing no damn — *dang* — graphic design. "Angelica, we both know I can't even stick-figure draw."

She stops craning her neck and we get on the back of the line, where I rummage through my bag.

"Your stick figures are beautiful. Don't hate on yourself. But no class can compete with the culinary arts class, right? That class was made for you."

When she sees me pulling out my phone, she presses her hand to lower mine. "Girl, what are you doing? The summer must have canceled your brain. You know your phone will get taken if a security guard sees you pull it out. They live for that shit."

" 'Buela has a doctor's appointment at four thirty and I may not have time to check in later. I just wanted to send a quick text to see how Babygirl's drop-off went."

Angelica changes sides with me to cover my body from any security guards or teachers who might be watching. The cafeteria ladies see me, but the only thing they care about is lunch portions and keeping the line moving. I check to make sure no one from the daycare called, send a text to 'Buela, and drop my phone back into my bag.

"Thanks for covering me."

"I'm going to need to you do the same thing when I send this thirst trap pic to Laura."

I shake my head with a smile. We pay for our lunch and make our way back to the table by the windows. One thing about Angelica: she's a pit bull once she sinks her teeth into an idea. And she's right back on discussing electives as soon as we grab a seat.

"Emoni, I see you doing that thing."

I groan and take a bite of my sandwich. I want to save my yummy applesauce for last. "What thing?" I say around a mouthful of turkey. If they put a little chutney on the bread, or a nice garlic spread and toasted it, this sandwich would be bomb. My fingers itch to take out my phone to write down a recipe idea.

"That martyr thing you do when you want something but convince yourself you can't have it because of Babygirl, or 'Buela."

I swallow. Is she right? Is that what I'm doing? Sometimes your girl reads you better than anyone else. "I just wish I had it figured out like you, Gelly. The girl-friend, the art school dreams, the grades."

She points her spork at me. "You're stronger than anyone I know, Emoni Santiago. It's senior year, the last time we get to just be teenagers. If you can't try something new now, when can you?"

"I don't know. Maybe. I'd like to learn how to cook food from Spain."

Behind her glasses, Angelica's eyes get wide. "Girl, you know it's not just learning to cook food from Spain, it's learning to cook food *in* Spain. My advisor told me there's a weeklong trip in the spring."

Schomburg has offered immersion classes before. A pre-Columbian history class that took students to an archeological site in Mexico, a fashion design class that took students on a tour of old textile mills in New England. There's never been a class I wanted to take, or a trip I thought I could afford.

And you have no business taking this class when you could have a study hall, and you can't afford this trip either, Emoni. But I don't say anything out loud to Angelica. I just take another bite of my sandwich, close my eyes, and savor, because I can't think of a single way to make my life more how I imagine it, but I can imagine a hundred ways to make this sandwich better. And sometimes focusing on what you can control is the only way to lessen the pang in your chest when you think about the things you can't.

KITCHEN SINK CONVERSATIONS

"Babygirl! You already look like you've grown!" I pick her up and twirl her around the living room.

'Buela swats at my butt with a dustrag. "Ay, Emoni, set her down. She just had some crackers." At that threat of throw-up, I settle Babygirl on my hip, even though she's getting heavier and I'm not getting any bigger.

"Did you learn a lot, Babygirl?" She nods and snuggles into my neck, still cradling her juice cup. I run my finger down her chubby cheek. My favorite silent game to play is to try and find my family in her features. Her big brown eyes and long lashes have to come from me;

42

'Buela has the same eyes. Her lips are the same shape as her father's. Aunt Sarah has shared some baby pictures of my mother and her as children, and I like to think I can see that lineage in her button nose, the seashell of her ears. And then there's the pieces of Babygirl that belong to her alone.

She pulls back from my neck suddenly and lowers her juice cup. "Chugga, chugga, choo-choo train!" she says. I look at 'Buela with a raised eyebrow.

"They read a book in daycare about trains. Mamá Clara says that Emma was very interested."

I nod at Babygirl as she garbles out a summary of the choo-choo trains book. At least, I assume that's what she's telling me.

"Don't you have a doctor's appointment?" I ask 'Buela when Babygirl is finished. "I thought I would find you running out the door. What's it for again?"

'Buela dusts off the family photos on the mantel. "My appointment got pushed back fifteen minutes, so I have a bit of time."

I notice she didn't answer the whole

question, but unlike Angelica, I know when someone wants a subject dropped. It was probably the gynecologist or something. And while 'Buela and I talk about everything, I'd really rather not know about her vagina. "Well, that's great. Babygirl, 'Buela or I will read to you tonight before bed. I think we have a choo-choo book around here somewhere." I set Babygirl down.

"No, not 'Buela. Tonight is bingo at the rec center. It's all you, Mommy."

I walk over and hook an arm across her shoulders. "Gonna go flirt with the cute bingo men?"

She shrugs my arm off and pokes me in the rib. "You always thinking about boys," she says, and I can't tell if she's serious or not, even though we both know that's not true. I ignore the tightness that immediately takes up space in my body. Although 'Buela never said anything to make me feel ashamed, I always wonder if she thinks I'm fast. If she secretly resents me for Babygirl.

'Buela must notice my stillness, because her face softens. "What are you going to make for dinner?"

The thought of cooking helps me let go of the mixed-up feelings inside. "I swear, you only keep me around for my cooking."

'Buela nods. "The only reason, of course. Glad you finally realized." But then 'Buela reaches out and grabs my hand. "Look how much you've grown," she says. "Did you learn a lot today?" That's 'Buela. Always cutting up the way only a Puerto Rican transplant to the hood can.

"You know how it is senior year; they're just trying to get us all through the door. Most exciting thing that happened is we get to pick new electives."

I turn on the TV to PBS and sit Babygirl on the couch with some toys and picture books. Take my shoes off and walk into the kitchen. The fridge is stocked — 'Buela must have gone grocery shopping this morning after dropping Babygirl off. We have iceberg lettuce (yuck) and bell peppers (yum), ground beef, onions. An idea begins taking root. I pull out the ingredients I need and rinse off my cutting board.

'Buela comes into the kitchen and

places her good hand against the counter so she's in the perfect position to watch me cook and also to peek into the living room and check on Babygirl.

"And so what class did you decide to take?" she asks me. I glance at her, unsure of her tone. She looks good in an Eaglesgreen sweater, cream dress pants, and her chanclas. Her pressed hair falls softly to cradle her brown chin. Her dark eyes, Babygirl's same eyes, my same eyes, are thoughtful.

I rinse off my favorite knife. "Um, I'm not sure. I had applied for study hall so I could get more homework done. With the new job and everything, free time on the weekend is going to be hard to come by." I chop the tops off the bell peppers and set them aside, move to slicing the onion.

"Well, that's very practical. How's Ms. Fuentes?"

"She's good." I should just let the subject drop since it's clear 'Buela means to, but then the words are out my mouth. "One of the classes that caught my eye was a culinary arts class."

'Buela reaches over and takes the knife from my hand. "You tell Ms. Fuentes I say hello. Work on the meat. I'll chop this for you."

"Dice it, please. Like this big," I say, and hold my fingers about three centimeters apart.

"And so, you want to take this culinary arts class?" she says, slicing the onion down the middle until she has two halves. I move away but watch her from the corner of my eye.

She stops mid-slice and holds the knife up. "Muchacha, I can chop an onion. Me vas a mirar the whole time I do it?"

I hold my hands up in surrender. Did I mention that my sous chef is temperamental? "Dice, 'Buela. Not chop. All the same size, please. And no, I don't know about the class. It sounds interesting, and I hear it includes a trip to Spain." I slide her a look. I try not to stare directly since I wouldn't put it past her to threaten me with the knife again for clocking her work. But I also don't know what she's going to say.

She cuts the onion carefully and quickly: my grandmother is a woman who is not afraid of tears or sharp things. "You wanted to go to culinary school

47

once, didn't you? A little late for that now, though."

I pause. Not sure what she means by "a little late" and not sure I want to find out. "Yeah, I guess. That was a long time ago. These days, I don't need anyone to stifle my creativity." Oregano, garlic powder, cayenne. The words ring in my head and, although I hadn't been planning on it, I grab some fresh ginger that 'Buela uses for tea. I pull some soy sauce packets out of a drawer we throw fast-food items in. "Put those onions in the pan with the olive oil, 'Buela."

"Sofrito?" she asks. But I'm not making the usual base.

"Something a little different this time." She tosses the onion into the oil, peels and crushes the garlic in el pilón, and then spoons that into the skillet, too.

"Bueno, I think you should take anything you want to take. As long as it doesn't distract you from school and your job. But an international trip, they usually have the students pay for those, right, nena? Is the trip required for you to take the class?" She walks to the sink and washes her hands.

48

I shrug, even though she has her back to me.

The oil pops out of the pan onto my palm. I realize I've had it on the heat for too long. I bring the spot where the hot oil landed up to my mouth and suck on the small ache.

'Buela gives me a little smile, then glances at her watch. "Okay. We'll discuss this again later. I'm off to Dr. Burke's. I don't know how I had too much time before and now I'm almost late! Where did the minutes go? I'll be back before bingo. Me guardas dinner."

CHEFDOM

Since my earliest memory, I imagined I would be a chef one day. When other kids were watching Saturday morning cartoons or music videos on YouTube, I was watching *Iron Chef, The Great British Baking Show,* and old Anthony Bourdain shows and taking notes. Like, actual notes in the Notes app on my phone. I have long lists of ideas for recipes that I can modify or make my own. This self-appointed class is the only one I've ever studied well for.

I started playing around with the staples of the house: rice, beans, plantains, and chicken. But 'Buela let me expand to the different things I saw on TV. Soufflés, shepherd's pie, gizzards. When other kids were saving up their lunch money to buy the latest Jordans, I was saving up mine so I could buy the best ingredients. Fish we'd never heard of that I had to get from a special market down by Penn's Landing. Sausages that I watched Italian abuelitas in South Philly make by hand. I even saved up a whole month's worth of allowance when I was in seventh grade so I could make 'Buela a special birthday dinner of filet mignon.

For my twelfth birthday she bought me a knife set — a legit, twelve-count knife set! — that no kid should probably have, but I watched YouTube videos and learned how to use those blades like a pro.

So, when we were applying to high schools in eighth grade, my middle school counselor asked me what I liked to do, and I told her I wanted to be a chef. I expected her to mention the magnet school with the most prestigious culinary arts program in the city. I'd already done some googling in the library and knew it was the best school around, with

restaurant-management classes and gas-
tronomics — all kinds of fancy courses.
And the counselor did mention the
school. As someplace I would have been
able to apply to if my grades had been
better. She told me she didn't think I'd
be able to test in. She enrolled me in the
lottery for Schomburg Charter instead,
even though their culinary arts program
wasn't well known, or even active at the
time. She said the school lottery was my
best hope to get into a competitive academic program.

'Buela prayed about that lottery for
weeks. Hundreds of students from all
over the city had their names thrown in,
and there were fewer than fifty spots
open for the incoming class. Out of all
the kids who applied from my middle
school and neighborhood, only three of
us were accepted: Pretty Leslie Peterson
from Lehigh Avenue, Angelica, and me.

See, I'm not a bad student; I'm just not
a great student. I feel like I need to do a
thing, and let my hands take over in
order for me to understand a subject.
When I'm in a class that has a lab or is
more hands-on, I'm good. But when it's

about memorization or recalling facts, I struggle. Even with extended time I don't always do well on tests. I'm lucky the teachers at Schomburg work with me to do additional projects that demonstrate I understand, but school isn't my thing at all.

And so, the closest I've gotten to chef-dom is making gourmet tacos for 'Buela and flipping burgers at the Burger Joint. And the one class I've most wanted to take hasn't been offered.

Until now.

THE NEW GUY

"Class, this is Malachi Johnson. He recently transferred here from Newark."

Amir in the back cracks his knuckles and I see some of the other dudes slouch in their seats. None of the guys likes someone messing up the vibe, especially not a dude from another city. The girls, though? We straighten up real quick. Well, not me. I'm not interested in a Malachi, Mala-can't, or a Mala-nothing. But he is a tall, dark-skinned dude, at least six foot four, and I already know he's a ball player and probably a *player* player from the way he walks — all swag and probably not one intelligent thought in his head. I look at my schedule. I've been going back and forth with the elective decision and Ms. Fuentes needs any changes by the end of class.

Ms. Fuentes clears her throat, and I look up from my list. She gestures to Malachi like she's that Vanna White lady from *Wheel of Fortune.* "Would you like to say a couple of words, Mr. Johnson?"

Malachi looks at her funny when she calls him "Mister," but he returns her smile. Angelica would say it transforms his face, that smile. He looks younger than seventeen, sweet, and like straight-up trouble. Some girl — or person (Angelica's always reminding me not to be "so damn hetero") — is going to find themselves caught up with Malachi. I can already tell.

He bounces one hand into the other and then shrugs. "Hey . . . thanks for having me. I've heard advisories are super-tight, so appreciate it." Oh, damn. I got it all wrong. Hearing him speak, I'm sure he's actually a nerd. Cynthia in the back giggles. Advisory just got a lot more interesting.

Ms. Fuentes beams at Malachi. "Great! You can grab a seat anywhere. You all go back to working on your essay prompt. I'll be coming around to conference with you about your schedules."

I finish filling out the elective sheet, then turn to the outline of my college essay that Ms. Fuentes assigned yesterday. I have a couple of ideas I might write about: having Babygirl and deciding to keep her. Or maybe what it's like to be raised by your grandmother because your parents aren't around. Maybe, what it feels like to get so focused in the kitchen that everything around me fades away. Ms. Fuentes says the topic should be "compelling," but how am I supposed to know what compels a college admissions person?

"Ms. Santiago, I'm so glad you've decided on the culinary arts class. It's perfect for you." Ms. Fuentes moves like a ninja. I didn't even hear her approach my desk, although I probably should have smelled her coming; her perfume has notes of lemon verbena. I love lemon verbena. Ingredients start arranging themselves on the kitchen counter in my mind and I can already taste an Emoni twist on 'Buela's tembleque recipe.

"Ms. Santiago, you heard there's an international trip opportunity as a component, yes? The teacher, Chef Ayden, has been planning all summer."

I snap out of coconut-pudding thoughts. "I heard." I don't want Ms. Fuentes to know that 'Buela and I are worried about the fee.

She moves closer to me. "You've talked so much in Advisory about how you love to cook. I think taking this class and traveling abroad will be an amazing opportunity."

I look around the room. Most of the other kids have their heads down but I know they're ear-hustling. Except for the new kid. He doesn't even have the decency to pretend he's not all in my business. He's found an empty seat by the sunlit window and is tapping a pencil on his desk, looking straight at me. When I catch his eye, he smiles shyly but keeps on staring.

I look away from him with a sharp cut of my eyes.

"Right, I hope the class will be great, Ms. Fuentes. Which one of these essay topics do you think I should write about?"

She holds my eyes for a long moment,

then she shakes her head and pulls her glasses off to peer down at my outline. "I think you should write about the one that scares you most. Taking risks and making choices in spite of fear — it's what makes our life story compelling."

There's that word again. She walks away but I have a feeling her advice wasn't about the essay prompt at all.

ON LOSS

What I remember: Tyrone is a pretty boy. Long lashes, slim, hair cut in a fade that was always Philly-sharp. We met at the beginning of my freshman year at a back-to-school turn-up in someone's basement. Although Tyrone went to school on the other side of the city, up by Mount Airy, where he lives, some of his middle school friends had ended up at Schomburg and it was a mix of kids at the party. Knowing what I know now, I'm surprised I was even invited, since there were barely any ninth graders there, but I think it was because some boy from Tyrone's school had been trying to get at Angelica. Tyrone was a year older and had a way with words. Pretty boys aren't usually my thing, especially one who expects you to worship the concrete he stomps on. I ignored him the whole party. This must have been a surprise to him because the next party, at the beginning of October, he was tripping over himself trying to get my attention.

Pretty Boy Tyrone of the pretty words took me downtown for our first date. We saw a romantic comedy that I thought was funny, but Tyrone kept huffing and puffing about how it was corny. We walked the streets of Love Park surrounded by trees and other couples. I remember I lied to 'Buela that night, told her I was hanging out at Gelly's house.

To this day I couldn't tell someone why Tyrone. Maybe because I didn't expect him to pick me. Maybe because most boys looked past my stick-board skinny body, more interested in the bubble-butt girls. Maybe because when I made him a cupcake he said it was too pretty to eat and waited a week, when the cupcake had gone stale, before taking a bite and still said it was the best thing he'd ever tasted; said it reminded him of a favorite birthday memory. Said he wanted to make me his girl.

"It" just seemed like what people were doing, and why not Tyrone? He was fine, older, and mostly nice to me. At least, I convinced myself he was nice. And most important, he wanted me. He could have sex with any girl, but I was the one he was after. Even thinking about it now I get a little twisted up inside. So much of my decision to have sex had more to do with being chosen than it did with any actual sexual attraction.

The day I lost my virginity, I had a half day at school and Tyrone skipped the rest of his classes to meet up with me. I was so nervous about a busybody neighbor seeing me bring a boy home that we went all the way to his house in Mount Airy while his parents were at work.

My first impression of sex? It was a lot more technical than I expected. He kept struggling with the condom and I laughed because I was nervous and he was fumbling so much. Apparently laughing is not the move at such a crucial moment, because his face got real tight around the mouth, and the fumbling got worse. And he was supposed to be the experienced one!

When he finally shoved into me, it stung. For a second I wasn't sure if I wanted to push him away or pull him closer, and then he was panting and sweating on my chest and apologizing. And I kept telling him it was okay, thinking he was apologizing for hurting me until I realized he was apologizing because it was over. I never even took off my bra. It didn't even last the entire Weeknd song playing in the background. A bubble of disappointment swelled in my chest and I didn't know if I was holding back laughter, tears, or a feeling I didn't know then how to name. All I could keep thinking was that he definitely didn't have any sweet words or niceness in the moment that I needed it most. I cleaned my own self up, put on my pants, and left. He didn't even say goodbye.

When I got home that afternoon, I peeled a ripe plantain. Its skin, dark as night, letting me know how sweet it would be. I sliced the plantain up into a dozen ovals, tossed them into a pan on the highest heat, and cooked them until they almost burned; the sugar turned bitter. I plated them with no accompaniment and I ate and ate until there was nothing left on my plate but a smear of oil.

It made me sick to my stomach.

To this day, whenever I've served someone maduros they end up crying, teardrops falling onto their plates for reasons they can't explain; and I can't eat them myself without weeping, without a phantom ghost pain twingeing between my legs.

Ever since Tyrone, I don't really talk to boys like that anymore. Boys at this age will say whatever they need to say to get what they want, and I've learned to trust pretty words even less than a pretty face.

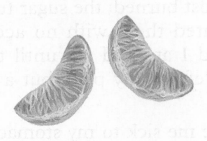

FAREWELLS

The first two days of school are over and done with, and before I know it, it's Saturday morning. Which means it's visitation time.

For almost the first two years of Babygirl's life, Tyrone's parents wanted him and Babygirl to get a blood test. But Tyrone knew I hadn't been with anyone but him and he never fought me on whether or not she was his daughter. Not that that mattered as long as he lived in his parents' house. He could come here and see her, and he has several times a month since the day she was born, but it's only been recently that he's been allowed to bring her into their house. It seems his parents were convinced by recent pictures that her features are starting to look more like theirs. He's taken custody every other weekend since the middle of summer and I'm still getting used to it. And she's still getting used to leaving. It's not fun for anyone.

Tyrone may be a lot of things, but at least he's present. And although he was never on time for a date with me, on the weekends he has to pick up Babygirl, he shows up like clockwork. Which is why I'm not surprised when he arrives at eleven a.m. on the dot on Saturday.

"Hey, Emma," he says, and crouches down with open arms.

"Daddy!" Babygirl sprints over and wraps her arms around him. He lifts her up and throws her into the air.

"You've gotten bigger in the last two weeks! You ready to see Grandma?" He holds her close when he speaks to her and she nods her freshly braided head. Tyrone's mom doesn't like seeing Babygirl in anything less than picture-perfect condition. Fuzzy puffs or "casual clothing" won't do. It's always a tight, clean hairstyle and Sunday-best-type clothes. She blinks up at her father like he's a burst of sunshine sliding through a window. I'm not jealous of that look, not at all.

Tyrone turns to me and grabs the outstretched baby bag. "I'll have her back right at seven tomorrow night. Anything I should know?"

I shake my head and lean in to give Babygirl a kiss on her cheek. Tyrone's cologne drifts around me and I have to stop myself from inhaling too deeply. Damn, he smells good as fu— hell . . . *heck*.

I take a step back and stop secretly sniffing him. "Her snacks are packed in her bag. So is her favorite picture book. Anything else just text me. I'll be at work this afternoon, but I can answer during my break. And 'Buela will be here all day. So you can call the house phone, too." I'm babbling. I hope he didn't notice.

Tyrone nods and bounces Babygirl against his chest. "You're babbling. You know we have her favorite snacks at my house, right, Emoni? You don't have to keep packing her juice boxes. And I know how to reach both of you." He bounces Babygirl some more and she squeals into his neck. I swallow back the lump in my throat. 'Buela stands in the kitchen doorway, circling her wedding band around and around her ring finger.

"Hey, Mrs. Santiago. How you doing?" Tyrone asks on his way to the door.

"I'm fine, Tyrone. Thank you for asking." 'Buela drops her good hand and walks with us to the front door. "Make sure to bring Baby Emma back in one piece," she says, and reaches out for Emma. Tyrone hands her over without a fuss and 'Buela gives her a long hug before putting her back in Tyrone's arms. "And you make sure to be a good girl for your father, okay?"

"Sí, 'Buela." Babygirl nods seriously. But I know what's coming.

We all smile. We open the door. Tyrone aims to walk through it, and just as he's about to pull the door shut behind him, Babygirl realizes what's happening. She's leaving. And 'Buela and I are not coming with her.

Her tiny face scrunches up and she begins screeching at the top of her lungs. I'm sure the row houses on either side of ours can hear her through the thick brick walls. Everything inside me wants to reach out, snatch her from his arms, and shut the door in his face, let her know I won't ever let anyone take her from me, but I force myself to be still. This has happened the other four times he came to pick her up. Tyrone looks at me and his full lips press into a thin line. He whispers to her quietly. I know from firsthand experience how Tyrone can sweet-talk a girl out of her fears, but his own daughter seems completely immune to his charm.

Babygirl continues trying to wrestle herself away from him, but he just keeps backing out of the door and whispering calming words. He scoops her bag more firmly onto his shoulder and strides down the steps. I watch as he buckles her into the car seat in his mother's expensive Lexus. When the car door shuts, I can't hear her crying anymore. Beside me 'Buela lets out a small sigh. We both watch through the open doorway until the car has pulled off and is out of sight.

"She's going to be fine, you know?" I say to 'Buela.

She nods and pulls me to her. "She's going to be fine," she says back to me. I inhale the scent of her vanilla perfume and begin the countdown until seven p.m. on Sunday. Only thirty-two hours to go.

I straighten up and blink away the tears in my eyes. I shut the door. "How about I make some tembleque? I was thinking of infusing the coconut with lemon verbena . . . and maybe vanilla. I have a couple of hours before my shift."

We walk with our arms around each other's waists into the kitchen.

LOVERS & FRIENDS

In the beginning, Tyrone and I tried to make our non-relationship work. After we found out about Babygirl, I mean. Truth is, Tyrone wasn't ever really trying to be with only me, and he didn't lie when he told me he didn't want anything serious. So after we found out I was pregnant we both felt kind of stuck. His parents kept telling him it probably wasn't his, that a fourteen-year-old who gets pregnant her freshman year probably had a few people she was letting scratch her itch. And I don't know that I could ever forgive that Tyrone barely defended me to them, even though he knew I was a virgin before him. Even still, during my pregnancy and after Emma was born, we played at being together.

And Tyrone *is* a good dad, but he gets to run away when he's done. During my pregnancy he never really could get why I was annoyed or got upset easily. Just told me to stop trippin'. And after Emma was born he kept wanting to fool around, apparently now because I had his kid it should be like that, but the two or three times we had sex I didn't feel good about it, and although I already had a kid, I still felt like we had to sneak around to do it.

So, what do you do with a guy who's eighteen and a better father than he is a boyfriend? I read a quote once that said, "The best thing a father can do for his child is love the mother." But some days I think the best thing Tyrone could do for Babygirl is leave her mother the hell alone.

RETURNS

On Sunday evening, 'Buela and I watch reruns of *Beat Bobby Flay* and eat her Fairhill-famous pernil and tostones. I was too jittery all day to cook and 'Buela has been too nervous to stand still. The whole weekend when I wasn't at work 'Buela and I have circled around each other, neither one of us wanting to say that we miss Babygirl. You'd think that finally having a day free would mean I would go out with Angelica or enjoy not having to be responsible for a whole other human, but instead it feels like a rip in the fabric of my life that won't get stitched back together until Babygirl walks through the door.

Babygirl gets home at 7:03, and 'Buela

is the one who answers the door in a mad rush and pulls her from Tyrone's arms. She passes Babygirl to me and I wrap my arms around her little body. Tyrone gives us a brief update before heading back to the car, but I don't hear a word.

"Mommy missed you so much, Mommy missed you so, so much," I say into her soft cheek. It's like our entire apartment had been holding its breath, but now that Babygirl's returned, even the breeze coming in through the window heaves a sigh of relief. 'Buela and I sit on the couch with Babygirl between us listening to her baby-sing about *Moana, PAW Patrol,* and cookies. Our dinner is forgotten; Bobby Flay is put on mute. For the rest of the night Babygirl is front and center, the candlelight we read the world by.

MAMA

It's a strange thing to become a mom when the only example you ever had wasn't even your own mother. Not that I don't think of 'Buela as my parent, but I also know that the way she raised me was different from how she raised my own father, that she thinks she failed by him and wants to make sure she doesn't fail me. That she's tired, and although she loves Babygirl, she wishes things could be easier for me. For us.

If I said I didn't have a ton of questions about my mother, I'd be lying. All the time I catch myself thinking: Would she be proud of me? If she were around, would I have gotten pregnant and had Babygirl? If she were still alive, would my father have stayed in Philadelphia?

From my mom's family I only keep in touch with her oldest sister, Aunt Sarah. She still lives in North Carolina and the only time I met her I was too young to remember: it was at my mom's funeral. We used to only talk during random phone calls around the holidays, but ever since she got a smartphone a few years back we've begun emailing once or twice a month. She sends me family recipes when she has a moment to type them out, although she cooks the way I do: no actual measurements, only ingredients and partial directions. When I remix the recipes and make them my own, I send them back to her so she can see how her niece hooked it up. She's invited me to come down south in the summer, but the summers are when Julio visits me, and after having Babygirl, I couldn't imagine traveling so far with her or without her. But I hold this connection close, since Julio never talks about my mother, and 'Buela just didn't know her well enough to tell me much. Sometimes Aunt Sarah's recipes will include a tidbit about my mother trying that food for the first time.

My mother's name was Nya, and I thought about making that Babygirl's middle name, but it didn't feel right, when I never knew her. I didn't know what kind of future I would be handing down to my daughter by pressing a name on her from the past. 'Buela raised me pretty superstitious about things like that.

Can you miss someone you never met? Of course, the answer is yes. I've made up a story about who my mother was, and I miss that person whether it's how my actual mom would have been or not. I imagine her patient, but strict. Someone who would paint her nails with me, and straighten my hair, and take me prom-dress shopping, but who would also demand good grades, and go to every parent-teacher conference, and wouldn't just say my food was good, but give me tough criticism.

On my bedside is a picture of my mother and father holding hands. He's wearing an Iverson jersey and she's in straight-leg jeans and a bright-blue T-shirt with a smiley face over her large belly. I'm the lump under the smiley face. It's the only picture I have of the three of us: my parents cheesin' and in love and holding hands, and me fully formed inside her belly, knocking on the door of skin, impatient to get out before everyone left.

NEW THINGS

The next morning, even though it breaks my heart, I say goodbye to Babygirl and rush out the door as 'Buela gets her ready for school. It's wild to miss someone so much, and yet in order to care for them you have to constantly say goodbye.

When I walk into Advisory Ms. Fuentes is passing out sheets of paper.

"Okay, on your desks you'll see your revised schedules."

Hmr — Advisory, Ms. Fuentes
Engl — Advanced English, McCormack
Math — Applied Math, Gaines
Soc — US Government, Ulf
For Lang — Latin III, Gatlin
Sci — Intermediate Physics, Ordway
Elec — Culinary Arts: Spain Immersion, Ayden

I was accepted into the class. The new boy, Malachi, stares out the window. I look back at the sheet. There's my name at the top. My other classes are the same. I try to keep cool even though I'm so excited my hands shake.

"You'll report for your first day of electives starting today. Let me know after class if you have any problems; now, take out the outline of your college essay. We still have fifteen minutes and we'll use them to revise the themes of your essays."

COLLEGE ESSAY: FIRST DRAFT

My father's name is Julio. And like the warm-weather month he's named after, he comes to visit once a year.

My grandmother says that my father couldn't handle being a single parent after my mother died. That before that, my mother kept him in check, but he'd had an itch under his skin to return to his island. My grandmother and grandfather moved when he was only fourteen, and they say he didn't adjust easily to the cold, the English, the way these streets were run so different from his own.

My grandmother chose to raise me when my father settled me onto her lap, asking her to watch me for a while, and then left the hospital. "A while" became seventeen years. It was in that exchange of my body from his hands to hers that the entire course of my life changed.

People say that you're stuck with the family you're born into. And for most people, that's probably true. But we all make choices about people. Who we want to hold close, who we want to remain in our lives, and who we are just fine without. I choose not to dwell on my father's rotating-door style of parenting, and instead reflect on my grandmother's choice to not only bring me home from the hospital and raise me, but also to offer me a fighting chance.

The world is a turntable that never stops spinning; as humans we merely choose the tracks we want to sit out and the ones that inspire us to dance.

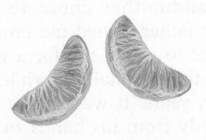

An Art Form

I try to keep myself from weeping when I first walk into the commercial-style kitchen. I've only ever seen a professional kitchen on TV and this one isn't nearly as updated, but it's still nicer than any kitchen I've ever been in. Against the far wall are two sets of double sinks and big metal cages full of mixing bowls, tongs, large wooden spoons, and serving utensils. Along the wall to my right are two full gas stoves and ovens. To my left, three massive fridges are framed by pantries that I assume hold dry ingredients. Pots and pans hang from the ceiling, hooked up like steel chandeliers. In the center of the room, five metal tables create a rectangle around a single table.

I've never been to an opera, but this

must be what it's like for a conductor to walk into an opera house, see the stage lit and the curtains drawn back, and know that they were meant to make the walls echo with music.

The instructor — I'm assuming Chef Ayden, since a chef's coat is buttoned neatly around the pudge of his stomach and he's wearing comfortable-looking checkered pants — walks out from his office in the back of the room just as Malachi rushes into class. For a second they stare at each other as the rest of us look between them. Chef Ayden isn't a tall man and has the kind of dark skin that's so free of blemishes it looks polished. Malachi walks to the only open spot next to Pretty Leslie, and for a second I think Chef Ayden is going to kick him out for being late. This boy *would* be in this damn class with me, and I don't know why it annoys me so much.

"This is not just another class. This is an actual kitchen. We have real knives, we have real food, and we have a real clock ticking on the wall that measures everything we can accomplish during a class period. And, as some of you might have heard, we have a real trip to another country planned for the spring. If you can't handle showing up on time to this class, I'm definitely not taking you abroad.

"I am not here because I always dreamed of being a teacher. I'm here because I love to cook, because you all had an opening for culinary arts in your school, and because I know how to run a kitchen. Before this is a school classroom it's a kitchen, and you all will respect it as such. Understood?"

He stops speaking, and clearly he means for us to answer. Some of us mumble, some of us nod. I wish I was in the classroom alone and could inspect the knives, and burners, and spice pantry.

He looks around the entire room, making eye contact with each of us before moving on. "Cooking is about respect. Respect for the food, respect for your space, respect for your colleagues, and respect for your diners. The chef who ignores one of those is not a chef at all. If you have a problem with respect, this is not the class for you. Please let me know and I'll sign the form for you to drop."

Chef Ayden looks around the room again but nobody moves. His eyes land on me and I hold his gaze.

"First things first: By the end of this week you'll have to fill out the loan form to borrow a chef's jacket and hat. When you walk into this room you aren't Schomburg Charter students — you're kitchen-staff-in-training."

I have a feeling that this dude has a lot of lectures he wants to give. Although I do like what he said about respect.

"Today you aren't even going to touch food." He waves a butter knife in the air. "Today you learn how to hold a knife."

I try to hold back a sigh that would rival any one of Angelica's, but it squeezes out my chest anyway and Chef Ayden's eyes zoom back my way.

For a second, when Chef was talking, I thought he must know what it's like in the places we're from. He sure sounded like he understood what it's like being from the city. But this butter-knife business lets me know he must be from somewhere else, because most of us in the room have probably been cooking and using knives our whole lives — not to mention we've seen them used on each other.

Everyone else must feel the same way because a couple of people shuffle their feet and Pretty Leslie clears her throat from across the room. "Um, Chef, I don't mean to be rude or whatever, but I thought this was a cooking class? I'm pretty sure most of us know how to hold a knife." *See?* Even Pretty Leslie feels me, and that girl is as contrary as I don't know what.

"Cooking class? No. *This* is a culinary arts class. As in, *this* is about creativity, and heart, and science — an art form. And no artist begins a masterpiece without understanding their tools and their medium. Anyone can teach you how to cook; you can google that. If you want to learn how to make art, stay here."

Pretty Leslie flips her hair and gives a small shrug, but she doesn't leave the classroom.

Neither do I.

MALACHI

"Hey, Santiago," a voice behind me calls. I look over my shoulder and see Malachi jogging up, narrowly avoiding bumping into a couple of football players. He doesn't even notice the way they grill him.

"Hey. Malachi, right?" I say. "You know you can call me Emoni? Only Ms. Fuentes does the last-name thing." I make sure not to slow down or change my walk in any way. I don't want this boy thinking for a second he's got any reason to talk to me.

Unfortunately, he has pretty long legs and it doesn't take much for him to keep up with my short ones.

"I don't think I knew that was your first

name. I like it. Isn't Imani one of the days you celebrate during Kwanzaa? I didn't think you were Black-black."

I can't help how hard my eyes roll. Here we go. "And why, Malachi, did you not think I was 'Black-black'?"

"Well, your last name is Santiago, you're light-skinned, and your hair's wild curly. I assumed you were Spanish," he says, pulling on a strand. I swat at his hand.

"Boy, don't touch me," I say. "My father is Puerto Rican and he's darker than my mom was, and her whole family is straight-from-the-Carolinas Black. And *her* hair was just as curly as mine. Not all Black women, and Latinas, look the same."

He throws his hands up in surrender mode. "My bad. Didn't mean to offend you none. I just wanted to know where you're from since you don't seem regular Black."

I take a deep breath. Because I know he didn't mean anything by his question. "I get you. And yes, I'm Black on both sides. Although my Puerto Rican side speaks Spanish, and my American side speaks English."

"I appreciate the race lesson."

He's trying to charm me. And I am not here for it. "Did you need something?" I ask, winding around a corner. Who made this boy think I had time for him? Got me out here wasting all my good words.

But then he smiles. Dimples popping out on both cheeks like billboards for joy and I stumble over my own feet. Shit, that smile should come with a trigger warning. Because *blao!* It's playing target practice with my emotions. It's even making me curse, and even though it's only in my head, I promised I would work on it. Now I'm really annoyed.

"Nah, Santiago. I just wanted to say hello. I'm glad we have this class together. I'd love to try your cooking."

I narrow my eyes at him. "Was that some weird sexual innuendo?"

His eyes widen and he barks out a laugh. "Dang, yo! I'm just trying to be nice. Get your mind out the gutter!"

"Oh, well, yeah. I guess tasting will be a part of the class." I stop in front of my English class. Angelica is sitting by the door and I see her already taking down notes. "This is me. . . ." And then because 'Buela didn't raise me to be rude, "Thanks for walking me to class."

"No problem, *Santi*."

BLACK LIKE ME

I've lived my whole life having people question what race I am. Not necessarily the homies I grew up with. In Fairhill, we are mostly Spanish-speaking Caribbeans and Philly-raised Black Americans with roots in the South. Which means, in my hood everyone's parents or great-grandparents got some kind of accent that ain't a Philly one. But when people from a different neighborhood first meet me, they wonder why I don't fit certain modes. The Latina grandmothers at the Papi store *tsk-tsk* when they ask me a question in Spanish and I answer with my chopped-up tongue, or worse, in English. And I don't have enough skills to tell them 'Buela didn't raise me speaking much Spanish. I can understand a lot of it because of her, but English is the language I learned at school and watched on TV and, for the most part, even the one we speak at home. I try not to be self-conscious about how little Spanish I know, but some days it feels like not speaking Spanish automatically makes me a Bad Boricua. One who's forgotten her roots.

But on the flip side, folks wonder if I'm Black American enough. As if my Puerto Rican side cancels out any Blackness, although if we go only according to skin, my Puerto Rican side is as Black as my Black American side. Not to mention, Julio may be a lot of things, but he sure is proud of his African roots and he's made sure I never forget our history. And 'Buela doesn't shy away from her Blackness either, even if she's quieter with how she talks about it. I don't know how many times someone has asked 'Buela for directions in the street and the moment they hear her accent a surprised "Oh, you Spanish?" slips out of their mouths.

I'm constantly having to give people

geography and history lessons on how my grandmother's hometown is 65 percent Afro–Puerto Rican, on how the majority of slaves were dropped off in the Caribbean and Latin America, on how just because our Black comes with bomba and mofongo doesn't mean it isn't valid. And it seems I'm always defending the parts of me that I've inherited from my mother: the roots that come from this country, the facts that Aunt Sarah tells me about our people in the Raleigh area, the little sayings she slips into her emails that I know come from her mother, and her mother's mother, and her mother's mother's mother, to the first African mother who touched foot on this here land. The same wisdom I whisper to Babygirl every now and then, a reminder of where, and who, we are from.

This stuff is complicated. But it's like I'm some long-division problem folks keep wanting to parcel into pieces, and they don't hear me when I say: I don't reduce, homies. The whole of me is Black. The whole of me is whole.

THE READ

"Who was that you were talking to?" Angelica pops a big wad of red gum into her mouth as the bell rings after English and everyone hustles down the hallway to their lockers.

"Who?" I ask, stealing a stick of gum before she can drop the pack back in her purse.

"Don't play dumb with me, Emoni," she says, poking me in the rib. "You don't talk to any of the guys at school and I definitely saw one fine-ass dude walk you to class. He new?"

Caught. "Oh, we have Advisory together and the culinary arts class. Malachi. Transferred from somewhere in Newark or something."

"Newark? Oh, he a brave soul bringing his ass over here. A very cute brave soul. . . . So, how did that class go? You seemed nervous when I saw you at lunch."

Angelica is looking at me, oblivious to the mob of lost-looking freshmen coming her way. I pull her to me so she doesn't get bumped. "It was okay. We talked about butter knives. Did you talk about tools in your art class?"

Angelica gives me a puzzled look before stopping in front of our locker. She turns the dial that opens up her top half.

"Tools? We went over the different design programs we'll be using. We won't start actual projects for a week or two while we learn the systems."

Huh. Maybe Chef was right; it's a different kind of tool, but sounds like Angelica wasn't just jumping right into design either.

"Tell me more about this Malachi person." She pulls her books out.

"Gelly, please. And move your big ole behind." I bump lightly against her and open my bottom locker. Put a textbook back and then shut it.

"I'm just saying. He would be a cute prom date," she says, popping her gum right in my face.

"And I'm just saying," I say, walking toward the school exit, "that unless they let in two-year-olds or middle-aged women, I don't plan on going to prom at all."

SALTY

"Welcome to the Burger Joint. What can I get for you, ma'am?"

"Well, let's see. What burger do you recommend?"

My manager, Steve, walks over, stands right at my shoulder, and immediately begins running his mouth. "All the burgers are delicious here, ma'am. You might want to try the Joint Special. It comes with extra bacon and cheese."

I think I should get points for the fact that I keep my face stoic. Steve is always trying to warm up to customers and jumping all in a cashier's space. I can feel his hot breath on my neck, and it takes everything in me to not shoot him the dirtiest look. Thing (1) That frozen slice of a mess infused with caramel coloring is *not* bacon. Thing (2) I don't know why anyone would want cardboard-flavored, fake-news cheese calories on their sandwich. Thing (3) If he wants to do my job for me, why did he hire me at all?

The woman nods along, then looks me straight in the eye. She seems like a professor. Her glasses sit low on her nose and she has the kind of presence that makes me thinks she's used to commanding attention in a lecture hall. "And you, young lady? What's your preference?" Her no-BS gaze never leaves my face.

I turn my lips up into what I hope is a believable smile. "The vanilla milkshake is good. It's made with real ice cream. And the number six is, um, popular?" I wasn't made for BS.

She nods again. "Thanks, honey. Not sure I'm craving a burger after all."

She walks out and a guy I know from school walks in. We aren't too far from Schomburg so I'm not surprised to see someone I recognize. I take his order and when I turn around to grab his fries, I bump straight into Steve.

"Sorry," I mumble, but he follows me into the prep area.

"Why didn't you back me up there, Emoni? We just lost money with that last customer."

"I just wanted to give her choices, Steve." I scoop some fries into a carton. The salt crystals gleam on them like some rapper's diamond-crusted chain.

Steve doesn't let it go. "You sabotaged a sale. You didn't even answer her question."

I give him a small shrug and what I hope is an apologetic smile. I load a tray with the fries and an apple pie, and walk over to the shake machine. Steve shuffles along with me. "What *is* your favorite sandwich, Emoni?"

Uh-oh. Girl, I do *not* eat the burgers here. I struggle to eat anything I can make 100 percent better in my own kitchen. But I need this job, so I quickly swallow and say, "I mean, everyone likes the number six, right?"

Steve narrows his eyes. "Emoni, I'm really going to need you to figure out how to be a team player. Or maybe this isn't the team for you?"

And with that, Steve huffs off to his office, his attitude as dry and stale as his fries.

TANTRUMS AND TERRIBLE TWOS

" ' "Have a carrot," said the mother bunny.' The end."

I close the picture book and kiss the top of Babygirl's head. She's snuggled against me with her thumb in her mouth.

"Babygirl, I told you to stop sucking on your thumb. It's a bad habit," I say, taking her hand in my own to get it away from her lips.

She waits a second after I let go before sticking her thumb right back where it'd been. "Read 'gain, Mommy." She speaks around the finger I gently pull from her mouth.

"Not tonight, babes. It's time for bed. Mommy has to do homework." I don't know what hit these teachers over the weekend, but every single one of my classes gave an hour's worth of homework today and I know I have a long night ahead of me. I swing Babygirl's legs around my waist and walk up the stairs to our room.

"I want read it 'gain!" she screeches, and I know she's going to interrupt the Eagles game 'Buela is watching. It's the first week of season games and 'Buela gets grumpy if she can't watch her team.

"Emma Santiago," I say, using her government name because it's the only way to get ahead of her tantrums. "Yelling won't work. I know you *want* me to read it again. But we've already read it three times and you have to learn you can't always get what you want."

Some days I'm convinced Babygirl has an old soul, the kind of spirit that makes me imagine she was meditating and holding yoga poses in my belly. I'm less convinced of that these days, when she's started spending more time away with her dad. I don't know if they're spoiling her over there, or have jumbled up her whole routine, but it sure is an adjustment to get her back to the Santiago way of doing things after the weekends she spends away. So when she starts wailing, crying, and throwing her stuffed animals out of her crib, all I can do is sigh and count under my breath.

"You were the same way, you know? When you wanted something, you let the whole world know."

I don't turn to 'Buela, who stands in the doorway. She doesn't enter the room. 'Buela lets me handle the tantrums by myself. At first, I used to get mad at her: What the hell did I know about making a baby stop yelling? But I've learned to appreciate her lack of intervention. She lets me be the mom.

"Babygirl," I say, walking up to the crib. "We can read the story four times tomorrow. I love that you love reading. But right now, it's time to go to sleep." She responds by throwing a doll at me.

"That's enough, Emma," I say. I don't use my no-nonsense voice often, but I bring it out now. "Just because you're angry doesn't mean you throw things at people."

She curls up, still crying loudly but clearly exhausted. Her small body heaves with sobs, and everything inside me wants to run my hand down her little head and just read her the damn story again. Just give her what she wants to stop her from hurting. But I keep still until she quiets down, until her breathing turns heavy. Once she's asleep I pick up the stuffed animals and place them neatly at her feet, then wipe the wetness off her cheeks. I turn her night-light on and close the door to our room. Thirty minutes wasted and it's all the bunny's fault.

'Buela follows me downstairs into the living room, where I replace *The Runaway Bunny* with *Applied Mathematics: Equations in the Real World.*

"I'm sorry we interrupted the game," I say, and sit on the couch.

"It was halftime, nena. And we are looking terrible; I sure hope my boys can get it together soon." She sits down next to me and removes the book from my hands. I sigh and put my head on her shoulder. She pats my face and I snuggle more deeply into her side.

"You want me to read to you?"

"I don't think the *Applied Mathematics* textbook will allow you to practice your character voices," I say, closing my eyes. She shifts a bit and I hear her pick up the book.

" 'Once there was a little bunny who wanted to run away.' "

FICKLE FATHERHOOD

My father has always loved to read to me. I may question a lot of his actions, but his phone calls from San Juan and his attempts to instill a love of knowledge into me aren't among them. Even my earliest memories include his voice in my ear reading a passage from whatever book he was currently into. Julio didn't believe in children's books. He believed whatever he read, he should read to me. Always nonfiction, and rarely fit for a child, but I loved listening to his voice.

These days, he doesn't read to me when he comes to visit, and he visits at the same time every year. Julio arrives at the beginning of July, usually with a full agenda. This past summer he rented a chair at the barbershop down the block and cut a couple of heads in the morning, volunteered at the cultural center in the afternoon, and attended summer lectures and readings at whichever one of the universities in the city was having an event.

Every day he invited me to come with him on his afternoon adventures, but I'm not one for lectures and my relationship with my father is complicated. Not to mention my new job didn't allow me to just drop work whenever he asked.

In the evenings, he was the perfect houseguest.

He helped wash the dishes even though he was always too late to eat dinner with us. He picked up 'Buela's medicine at the pharmacy or anything we needed from the grocery store. He played with Babygirl and pretended he was going to buzz-cut her hair until she squealed with laughter and batted at his clippers. He was one of the few people who could stop her from crying when she was throwing a tantrum. I had a glimpse into the kind of father he might have been if my mother had lived.

If he had chosen to stay.

But Julio never stays long and he never gives notice. At some point when August starts rearing its head, Julio begins rearing his toward a flight back to Puerto Rico.

At the end of July this year, when 'Buela and I got home from the supermarket, all his stuff was gone from the living room. His suitcase wasn't in the corner. His blanket was neatly folded over the couch. The case with his barbering tools was nowhere to be seen. Babygirl was at Tyrone's house that weekend, so not only did he not say goodbye to us, he didn't even say goodbye to her. And by that point she'd gotten attached to "Pop-Pop," as she called him.

But *poof*! Houdini in the flesh. Or rather, in the disappearance. He didn't leave a note, he didn't text goodbye. He called a week later like nothing had happened and asked if I could send him Angelica's Netflix password so he could watch a documentary on the Young Lords.

And maybe because I struggle to learn

certain lessons, this one has taken me years and years to learn: You can't make too much space for a father like mine in your life. Because he'll elbow his way in and stretch the corners wide, and when he leaves all you have is the oversized empty — the gap in your heart where a parent should be.

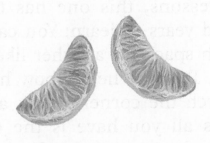

EXHAUSTION

"Santi, you were really quiet in Advisory today," Malachi says. I don't know when he decided he had a right to nickname me. But I'm too tired to correct him. It's only the middle of the second week, and although we see each other in class, we haven't spoken much.

"Yeah. I was up late doing work. And Ms. Fuentes gave me a shi — crapload of edits on the college essay draft."

He raises a questioning eyebrow at my curse correction, but drops it. "What are you writing yours on?" he asks.

I cut around the corner on my way to my next class. "We don't have Cul Arts until later in the day, Malachi; where are you going?"

"Just walking you to class, Santi."

I stutter to a stop near a water fountain. "Malachi, we aren't friends. We can be friendly, but I don't want you to get it twisted. I know you're new and I'm not trying to be mean. But I just want to be clear . . . we, you and me? Aren't friends."

I wouldn't always have been able to say that to someone. I was so quiet and shy and surprised to get any attention at all. But the toddler books all suggest moms practice direct and clear language, managing expectations, giving explicit instructions, et cetera. Sometimes I think boys are just like babies when it comes to something they want — and they need to be told *no,* firmly and without qualification.

Malachi reaches up and pulls on one of my curls. "Okay, Santi. We aren't friends. Can I walk in the same direction as you until you get to your class?"

"Won't you be late for yours?"

He shrugs. " 'We, you and me, aren't friends,' so don't you even worry about my attendance record, Santi." He flashes his smile, and at the sight of his dimples I almost melt. "Plus, you are one of the few kids I've had actual conversations

111

with. Why don't you tell me some things I should make sure to see in the city?"

And although I don't want to encourage Malachi more than necessary, I'm always looking for a reason to big-up my city. "Well, let's start with cheesesteaks. The spot all the tourists go to? Basura. The best cheesesteaks . . ."

A Tale of Two Cities

I come from a place in Philadelphia that reminds me of a Charles Dickens book we read in English. The *Tale of Two Cities* one that's set in Paris and London during and after the French Revolution. But the place I come from ain't nowhere close to Europe. I'm from Fairhill. It sounds pretty, don't it? And for a lot of outsiders, the name is the only pretty thing about it.

Most folks are Puerto Rican. Julio tells me this neighborhood has the highest rate of Puerto Ricans outside of the island. I don't know why, though. It doesn't look anything like pictures of the island I've seen. Blocks and blocks of two-story row houses, concrete, fenced-in yards, and vacant lots. People have had a lot to say about our neck of the woods, but in general, they should probably keep their neck out our business. This part of North Philly has one of the highest crime rates in the city, or at least that's what the newspaper reports. They call us part of the Badlands, but when you stay here, you know there's a lot more goodness than is reported in the news.

Sure, we have gang fights that happen to the soundtrack of gunshots, but we also have dance crews that perform at the summer block parties. We have el Centro de Oro, the strip of Puerto Rican shops where you can get everything from oversized flags to island spices to hand-carved mortar and pestles. We have corner-store owners who hand out candy during Halloween, and the barbershop on the block that keeps a cooler of cold water out front in the summer. We got the rec center where most of us grew up doing our homework, where I received teen-parenting classes and counseling while pregnant, and we got the cultural center a few blocks over that has art workshops, free English lessons, and even brings in live bands for concerts.

Maybe it's more than just a tale of two cities; it's a tale of two neighborhoods. On the one hand, people are scared to come over here because they say this part of town is dangerous, "undeveloped," and a part of me thinks, good, keep out, then. But everyone knows that the good things like farmers' markets, and updated grocery stores, and consistent trash pickup only happen when outsiders move in. And as much as it seems our neighborhood is forgotten, change is coming. I've been seeing more and more construction sites and lots of houses with *SOLD* signs, and more than ever before white people have been getting off at my train stop, eating at Freddy & Tony's, wearing their fancy college sweaters and looking like they are nervously making their way home. Home. I come from a place that's as sweet as the freshest berry, as sour as curdled milk; where we dream of owning mansions and leaving the hood; where we couldn't imagine having been raised anywhere else. People wonder why I walk so hard, why I smile so rarely at strangers, why I mean mug and carry grit like loose change in my pocket.

And everyone in Philadelphia reps their hood just like me. One of the first things you ask and learn about someone is where they stay. Where we come from leaves its fingerprints all over us, and if you know how to read the signs of a place, you know a little bit more who someone is.

And me? I'm pure Fairhill, but I also got more than one city, one hood inside me. And anyone who wants to get to know me has to know how to appreciate the multiple skylines.

FAIL

"Under what conditions do pathogens that contaminate food grow?" Chef Ayden scans the room. "Sharif?" Sharif looks down at his station as if the answer is written in magical ink. He shrugs. Chef Ayden makes a note on his clipboard. Today we were surprised with a verbal pop quiz. In addition to studying the components of a recipe, learning to plate, and learning to serve, Chef Ayden also wants us to prepare for the ServSafe test. He rarely quizzes us like other teachers, with a written-down test. Instead he asks questions out loud and you have to be quick on your feet. He says being able to respond quickly and efficiently is how it will be in a real kitchen. And although we hate the quizzes, we all want to pass the ServSafe test. If we pass that test, not only do we pass the class, but we are also given a certificate by the city that proves we know how to safely handle food and can work at a restaurant. Technically, with that certificate I could apply to take over Steve's job at the Burger Joint. I don't *want* Steve's job, but I like knowing I have the credentials to take it from him if I wanted to.

"Emoni."

I stop tucking away the ends of my head scarf. Chef said I could wear this instead of a hat as long as it keeps my hair out of my face and my pots. My curls were not fitting under that hat. "Yes, Chef Ayden?"

"At what temperature is chicken considered time-temperature abused?"

My eyebrows shoot up. I hadn't paid attention to the temperature portion of the study guide. . . . Chicken is done when it's done.

"Emoni?"

I close my eyes. "When you cut the chicken, you want the inside to show only the slightest hint of whitish-pink, since the chicken will keep —"

He makes a note on his clipboard. "Emoni, what pieces of information need to be on the label of food you plan to store in the freezer?"

"The expiration date. I mean, the date the food was prepared. And the time the food was prepared. The name of the food?"

I look at the spot right over Chef's shoulder; I can't meet his eyes. He makes another note on his clipboard. "You're not wrong. But you're also not technically right. You have a sense of what works. You understand it in practice. But you still need to learn the technicalities. Cooking is a science; it's more than just instinct."

Although I want to drop my head, I keep my chin up. This is exactly what I was afraid of, that this class would be more about what I could memorize than what I could do. Most of us signed up for this class to travel and cook, and we haven't discussed either.

Chef Ayden seems to be waiting for me to say something, but I just stare at him silently. He shakes his head. "Leslie, talk to me about storing food. Where is the safest place to store dry goods?"

And when the attention swings to Pretty Leslie I finally drop my gaze, shame like the bacteria Chef Ayden asked about spreading under my skin.

CATHARSIS

'Buela comes into the kitchen and turns on the radio. The sound of Marc Anthony wailing alongside an orchestra fills the kitchen. I would wrap my soul in a bow and sell it with the quickness to be able to cook for Marc Anthony. That man can *sing*. 'Buela pulls out the herbs that she gets directly from el campo in Puerto Rico and sets them on the counter. The sweet-smelling yerba buena, the Caribbean oregano. She hands me the knives before I ask for them, cleans the cutting board before I realize I need it rinsed.

Some days, when my feelings are like this, like a full pot of water with the fire

121

on high, I don't know what to cook. Plans and ideas escape my mind and instead I let my heart and hands take control, guided by a voice on the inside that tells me what goes where.

I push aside, or maybe I push forward, all the things I feel. Angry that I have to give Babygirl away every other weekend. That I have to dress her like a doll for her grandmother to love her. Conflicted about this damn elective that I convinced myself to take and that has now become my toughest class. Upset I have a greasy-ass job serving some cookie-cutter food where I get in trouble for the smallest mistakes. Confused about a father I love but also miss. Nervous that it's senior year and I don't know if college is in the plans for me. And I don't know what is in the plans if not that.

My hands move on their own, grabbing and slicing and mincing. And 'Buela and I are making music alongside the radio, the clanging of pans, the mortar against the pestle, our voices humming.

When all the sounds stop, including the radio, it's like I'm waking out of a fog. The stove is turned off. 'Buela wipes down the counter and folds the dishrag before turning to me. I lift the pot lids and see that I've made a fragrant yellow rice with cilantro. Somehow, black-eyed peas found their way into the rice, but I can tell from the smell that it works. The chicken looks juicy, and smothered in onions, it's cooked perfectly *without a thermometer.* The green salad with a spinach base is crisp. Not a complicated meal, but one made for comfort.

I plate 'Buela's portion using one of the lessons I learned from the cul-arts textbook: the starch on the bottom and the protein on top, sauce spooned over both; a separate bowl for the salad.

After the first bite, she closes her eyes, and when she opens them, she is in tears. She laughs when she wipes her eyes. "Look at me crying! Like this doesn't happen every time, nena."

I don't often ask questions about how people react to the food I cook. It makes my belly squeeze tight to know my dishes might have an effect I don't mean them to have; like something inside me left my body and entered into the pots and pans without a permission slip. But today I need to know. "What did it make you feel, 'Buela?"

She squeezes her napkin in her hand and doesn't look at me as she moves her fork around the plate with the other. "It brought back a memory of being a little girl and staring out at the ocean. And wanting so badly to jump right in and swim far, far away, and being scared that if the water ever went above my neck it would swallow me whole and never spit me back out."

I nod and take a bite of my own food. No memories spring up, no new feelings. The only thing that happens is my taste buds respond to the tangy and salty notes.

"Even that memory, of longing for what I was afraid of, warms me up. Like a candle being lit from the inside. You were given magic, nena."

I let go of a breath I didn't know I'd been holding. I don't know much about pathogens and storing sugar, but damn if I don't know how to cook good food that makes people hungry for more, that makes people remember food is meant to feed more than an empty belly. It's also meant to nourish your heart. And that's one thing you won't ever learn from no textbook.

PUDDING WITH A POP

What they don't tell you about a culinary arts class is that it's a lot of work. More than when you cook in your own kitchen. We meet three times a week, on Monday, Wednesday, and Friday. And now that the introductory classes are done, each class is supposed to be broken down into a different category: demonstration day, when Chef Ayden teaches us a new skill and we practice it; recipe day, where Chef Ayden leads us through a new recipe; grading day, where we have to follow the recipe on our own and get graded. Technical quizzes happen at the top of every class as we prepare for the ServSafe test. But we've yet to make a recipe on our own.

And so, for the last two weeks, second-to-last period every other day I walk into the kitchen, button up my white jacket, put my hair up in a pineapple, and tie on my head scarf, ready to get to my burners. But honestly, we spend more time cleaning than we ever spend cooking. We are always washing our knives, wiping down our cutting boards, clearing our stations, sanitizing our areas, putting things away from drying racks. It's exhausting work and I know, like me, some of the other seniors were hoping for an elective that was going to be a little less intense. We've already had two people drop the class; both Sharif and a girl named Elena decided they'd rather have a study hall, so now our class is only a tiny group of ten.

Although I dread the quizzes, which are on everything from serving food to preparing it, I like the bits and pieces we learn about running not only a kitchen but a restaurant. I would hate to make someone sick with my food, and that's what I try to remember when I'm studying for quizzes. But I just want to get to the part I'm good at: cheffing it up.

And today, for the first time, we are given a real recipe: making chocolate pudding from scratch. We stir cocoa and cornstarch and sugar together, then stir in milk. Chef guides us step by step and we all clean our stations as the pudding chills. As I'm putting away my ingredients, a little red bottle in the pantry calls my attention. I snatch it up and sprinkle some on my pudding. When Chef Ayden calls us up to test our dishes, I'm the first student to set my bowl in front of him. He grabs a clean plastic spoon and pulls my dish closer to him, leaning down to inspect it, turning the dish slowly in a circle. "Mmm. Nice chocolate color, smooth texture; you made sure the cream didn't break, which is great. And I'm curious what this is on top."

He takes a tiny spoonful and pops it into his mouth, and the moment his mouth closes around the spoon his eyelids close, too. I wonder if my cooking woo-woo will work on him. "What is that?" he asks, his eyes still closed. I assume he means the spice on top and not whatever memory may have been loosened by my pudding. His eyes open and I realize the question was in fact for me.

"I used a little smoked paprika," I say.

Heat creeps up my neck. I hadn't even thought about what would happen if I used an ingredient that wasn't in the original recipe.

"You trying to show off, Emoni?" Chef Ayden asks me very, very seriously.

"No, Chef. I wasn't."

"The ancient Aztecs too would pair chocolate with chipotle and cayenne and other spices, although it is not so common now. Why'd you add it?"

"I don't know. I saw it in the pantry and felt the flavors would work well together."

He takes another spoonful. Chef told us from the beginning that since every student is evaluated, he would very rarely take more than one bite of any single dish. I'm surprised he does so now, but he closes his eyes again as if the darkness behind his lids will help him better taste the flavors. His eyes pop open.

"This isn't bad." He drops his spoon. "Emoni, I think creativity is good. And this, this . . ." He gives a half laugh like he's surprised he doesn't know what to say. He clears his throat and it seems almost like a memory has him choked up. "This is delicious, but I want to make sure you follow the ingredients list. If you work under a chef and they give you clear directions, it's disrespectful to try and modify their recipe without first consulting them. Whether or not you think the flavors will work."

He takes another spoonful of my dish. "Class! Everyone grab a spoon. Come eat Emoni's chocolate pudding." A couple of the boys begin snickering and I know they took his comment the dirty way. I don't drop my head, but I'm blushing and it's from a mix of both pride and embarrassment.

When we leave Culinary Arts, Malachi runs after me.

"Yo, Santi, you should have seen your face!" Malachi laughs.

Although class ended several minutes ago, I'm still flushed. "I can't believe he said that like he didn't know y'all got nasty minds!"

Malachi laughs again. "I don't think Chef sees humans when he looks at us, only white jackets and chefs-in-training." He lowers his voice. "And to be fair, it was really very good pudding."

I swat him on the arm. "Stop that. Oh my God, I can't go back there."

He laughs again. "You'll be fine."

"You have a nice laugh," I say, and I must look as surprised as he does that the words left my mouth. "We're still not friends. I don't know why I said that."

"Thank you. You have a nice laugh, too, even though I rarely hear it."

"Don't say thank you. And don't pay it back. That wasn't a compliment. It was an observation."

Malachi shrugs and calls over his shoulder, "I won't, Santi. And I haven't laughed that much in a while. So thanks for that, too."

LIVING LARGE & LAVISH

On the bus ride home after school, Angelica is listing all the schools with graphic design programs she wants to apply to: NYU, Pratt, Savannah College of Art and Design. I listen quietly as she lists all the pros and cons of each program and the different professors she wants to work with at each school.

"I just don't know if I'll get in. All of these programs are amazing. They only accept the best of the best."

I shake my head. "Gelly, are you crazy? You are an incredible artist. Why do you think the school always asks you to draw the sports posters and decorate for the school dances? Why do all the kids in our class ask you for help whenever they need something designed? You see the world like no one else. Those schools should kiss your feet for even applying."

And I'm not just blowing smoke up Angelica's ass. I mean, tush. Whether it's designing an outfit, drawing a logo, or putting together a flyer, if you give that girl a colored pencil, she'll give you back something that belongs in an art gallery.

"I guess. The guidance counselor thinks I have a good shot, and my mentor at the museum says my portfolio is the shit, but I'm nervous. What about you? What schools has Fuentes thrown your way?"

I stare out the bus window. "Fuentes knows any school I apply to will have to be in Philadelphia. She's had me research La Salle, Temple, St. Joseph's. She's pushing for Drexel, which has a culinary arts program, but you know I'm not good at school, so a scholarship is out the question. I don't even want to think about taking out loans. And how can I work full-time and go to school full-time and raise Babygirl full-time? I think in order of most important, school is at the bottom, right?"

I tap my fingers against the window-pane and fight the urge to bite on my nails.

Angelica is quiet for a long moment and I'm thankful she doesn't rush to re-assure me with unrealistic words. "But what if you get financial aid? You can't just work at the Burger Joint full-time."

"It's not a bad job. It pays me and I can maybe make manager one day."

But how can I give Angelica an answer when I don't know myself? I stop staring out the window and force a smile. "Right now I'm going to keep working on your anniversary menu. How do you feel about lobster? Super romantic."

She shakes her head. "Okay, girl. I'll drop the topic. But just know, I think you have more to offer the world than you give yourself credit for."

I look at Angelica and smile. "Same, sis. Borrow that same advice. If one of those schools will make you a stronger artist, fill out the application and shoot your shot. For you, the stars and be-yond."

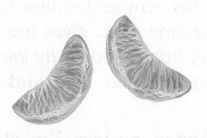

IMPOSSIBILITIES

It's Wednesday and we are working on a new recipe. I'm glad a week has passed and people have stopped asking to taste my pudding. I tuck the ends of my scarf in. Putting on my jacket and head wrap always makes me feel like I'm a ball player in my full uniform stepping onto the court.

"Today you're working with saffron. This isn't a regular spice; it stains and it's costly. A friend brought it back to me from Europe, so be precise with your knife work. Find a classmate; there's not enough to go around to do this individually." Chef Ayden claps his hands together.

I look around the room as people pair up. At Malachi's station, Pretty Leslie squeezes his arm and smiles up at him. He catches my gaze, gives me a player's shrug like, *I don't know why the pretty girl keeps touching me,* and looks back at Leslie.

Chef Ayden notices I'm still alone. "Emoni, it seems we have an odd number in class today. Will you work by yourself, or do you want to join another team and make a threesome?" I shake my head. Chef Ayden keeps putting me in the most awkward situations with his comments. I can't even be mad at the snickers.

"I'm fine working on my own."

Chef Ayden wasn't wrong. It does take almost the entire period, and we have only ten minutes left to plate our rice dishes and taste test.

"Good job, class. The chorizo on your cutting board wasn't the highest quality, but when it is, this paella is really something special, and a staple in most Andalusian homes." He clears his throat. "I have an announcement to make."

We all look up. Dang, is he quitting already? It's only been three weeks.

Chef is still talking. "As you all know from the course description, we are set to travel to Sevilla, Spain, for spring break in late March." My heart begins beating fast. For years, I've watched reruns of Anthony Bourdain shows where he tries food from all over the world. I've listened to chefs on *Chopped* talk about training in Paris and London. I've imagined myself traveling to far-flung places that have ingredients I didn't know existed.

"I didn't want to bring it up until we had the budget confirmed. The administration has returned with the initial numbers and I now have a sense of what each student needs to raise. Each of you is accountable for eight hundred dollars by December fifteenth in order to attend the trip. We will, of course, plan fund-raisers to help reduce that cost."

An ache shoots from my heart. Eight hundred dollars in what, a little over two and half months? I won't work enough hours to make even half of that by the deadline. Sure, some kids will be able to afford that without a fund-raiser: Amanda, whose parents own a small accounting firm in Port Richmond. Talib, who stays over in Chestnut Hill with his lawyer father. I know for sure I, and probably Pretty Leslie who's from the same hood, can't just come up with eight hundred dollars, money that would be better going toward the light bill and groceries or new shoes for Babygirl.

A week in Spain would change my life; it'd be huge, it'd be amazing . . . it'd be impossible. My stomach feels twisted in knots. I want to go so bad, but I grab that hope between my fingers and crush it like the strands of saffron, praying it doesn't leave a smudge.

SANTI

I'm one of the slowest students to clean my station, and when I leave the class-room Malachi's leaning against the wall talking to Pretty Leslie. She giggles at something he says, but as if he feels me watching, his eyes swing my way. I raise an eyebrow and scoot past them.

"Hey, Santi," Malachi says.

I don't want to be rude, but I also don't want to talk to Pretty Leslie, so I shake my head and keep going.

"Santi, I want to ask you something."

I stop in the middle of the hallway and wait for him to catch up. He takes his sweet time walking over, Pretty Leslie on his heels.

"Wassup?" I say. I give Pretty Leslie a

head-nod and she looks between Malachi and me, her perfectly penciled-in eyebrows furrowing.

"I'm good, Emoni. How are you?" She pops her gum, then lowers her voice in a fake whisper. "How's your daughter?"

I force myself to keep smiling. I'm not ashamed of my baby. I'm not ashamed I had a baby. I'm not ashamed I'm a mother. I lift my chin higher. "Babygirl's real good. She just started daycare little over a month ago. Thanks for asking."

I look Malachi straight in the eyes. His dimples are gone.

"That's wonderful!" Leslie says. "I don't know how you do it, girl. I couldn't imagine being a parent in high school. Right, Malachi?"

But Malachi isn't listening to Leslie. His eyes are on me. If there was one thing I learned once my belly started showing it's that you can't control how people look at you, but you can control how far back you pull your shoulders and how high you lift your chin. Boys think of only two things when they find out you had a baby: thing (1) that you're too much baby-mama drama, or thing (2)

140

that you're easy. Malachi pushes off the wall, but I keep myself as still as a dancer waiting for her cue before she spins.

"You called my name because you wanted to ask me something?"

"Santi, do you like ice cream?"

I glance at Pretty Leslie. She looks as surprised as I feel. "Uh, ice cream?"

"I have a craving for ice cream. If you're not busy after school, you want to get ice cream?"

He's the most serious I've ever seen him. I look between him and Pretty Leslie. The fake sweet smile she was wearing has cannonballed clear off her face into a pool of confusion. Is Malachi asking me on a date? In *front* of Pretty Leslie?

"I mean I know we're not friends, or whatever." He smiles. The playful gleam is back in his eyes. "But I was hoping we could talk."

I let go of the breath I didn't know I'd been holding. "I'll meet you at the main entrance after the bell."

And even though 'Buela raised me right, she didn't raise me to be nobody's punk, so I don't bother saying sh— *ish* to Leslie.

And damn if I don't have a little swag in my step as I walk to English.

THREE'S COMPANY

"Hold up, wait. Run that back for me. That bitch Pretty Leslie tried to basically out you to this guy and then he played the shit out of her and asked you on a date? In front of her? I need to meet this dude ASAP."

I laugh at Angelica and grab my sweater from my locker. The weather is definitely cooling down — finally — and the last thing I need is a cold. "She didn't try to 'out' me. I'm not a closet mom. And your language, Gelly!"

Angelica slams the locker shut. "Don't try to censor my language, Emoni, just because you slipped in front of Babygirl. But seriously, he didn't know, right? So it was your story to tell, not hers."

"I don't even know if she did it on purpose. Maybe she was trying to be nice."

Gelly hooks her arm through mine. "Emoni, not even you are that naive. Didn't I raise you better? She was trying to piss on him."

"Gelly! What are you saying? Make a right." We turn.

"You know exactly what I'm saying. He was a fire hydrant and she was marking her territory, but instead the fire hydrant picked up legs and walked up under your tree."

Gelly and her vivid imagination. "I don't think that extended metaphor is working for you."

Angelica screws her forehead up thoughtfully. "No? I think it would make an interesting painting. Where are we going again? Why'd we turn this way?"

But we're already at the main entrance and there's Malachi. Standing with a group of other guys, all of them laughing. How does he make friends so fast?

Angelica takes one look at him and her eyebrows lift into her bangs. "Isn't that the cutie I saw walking you to class? Is *that* Malachi? Is that why we came this way? Get it, girl!"

I pinch the inside of her arm to hush up any more questions.

Malachi notices us and daps up the other dudes before breaking through the circle to approach me.

"You actually came. There is hope in the world," he says, smiling. Then he turns to Gelly, just like that, not even waiting for an introduction. "I'm Malachi. I transferred from Newark."

Angelica's eyebrows are still raised high on her forehead when she looks at him. "Hello, Malachi. I'm Angelica. What's your business with my friend?"

"It's funny you should ask. Why don't you come with us for ice cream and we can discuss. Is there somewhere near here we can go?"

Angelica and I look at each other. There's no ice-cream spot nearby. And neither one of us would want to hang out so close to school anyway. There's only one place to go.

"You ever hung out by the Schuylkill?" I ask.

We cross the street to the train station on Broad Street. The walk is a silent one and I begin getting nervous about Malachi and Angelica having an awkward conversation. If he says something wrong, Angelica won't hesitate to tell him about himself.

But as soon as we get on the train, Malachi asks Angelica a million questions about me, and that traitor starts telling him all my embarrassing middle school stories. I'm glad the train is so packed people can't overhear their conversation or see my blushing cheeks. Angelica asks him about his intentions again, but it's clear she's mellowed out some and Malachi's small shrug and sweet smile seems to be answer enough for her. We transfer to a second train and it takes us another twelve minutes to get to the right stop, then a five-minute walk toward the boardwalk to find the water-ice shop Angelica and I love.

"This isn't ice cream," Malachi says when we step into the shop.

"No, it isn't. It's better," Angelica

answers. We both look at him, daring him to argue that water ice isn't a direct gift from the gods.

Malachi is clearly an intelligent guy because he knows better than to say a word. He just orders his lemon-flavored ice and we walk to the water. It's a beautiful day and the way the light hits the water makes me so grateful to be where I'm from. I look at the bridge, the city skyline, people in canoes on the water, kids splashing in and out of a sprinkler nearby.

Angelica spoons some cherry ice into her mouth and breaks the silence. "How are you two liking the culinary arts class?"

Malachi carefully eats some of his water ice. "I like it. Has Emoni told you about the time we all licked her pudding?"

Angelica shoves her red bangs out of her eyes. "Hold up, what?"

I swat Malachi on the arm. "It just sounds dirty."

"Ouch. You're heavy-handed. I'll add that to the list of things I've learned about you today."

We all get quiet. Then Angelica smiles brightly. "Well, I'm going to go meet up with Laura. Her school is right around here and it should have just let out. Emoni, give my goddaughter a hug for me. Malachi, make sure you get her home safe." She points at him as she gets up. "And don't make me hunt you down."

He holds his hands up in surrender. "Yes, ma'am. I will treat her like the friends we aren't." He smiles wide. And I see Angelica falter. Angelica, who doesn't even blink twice over Idris Elba, almost trips on herself at the sight of Malachi's smile. I see the artist in her spark to attention.

"What a beautiful smile," she says softly, like she's talking more to herself than to him. "This one, the real smile you have on right now. Almost as if you're choosing to give a sunlit middle finger to this fucked-up world." She reaches out a finger and taps one of his dimples, softly. "Be careful with that smile." She raises an eyebrow and looks my way; clearly the warning is for me.

Gelly twinkles her fingers goodbye as she leaves.

When I turn to look at Malachi the smile is gone. The silence grows heavy.

I throw my empty cup into a nearby trash can and wipe the sticky juice off my fingers with an extra napkin. "She didn't mean anything by that. And she doesn't like guys, so don't take the dimple touching too seriously."

"You sure? I think I felt some serious vibes coming my way." But I can tell he's joking.

"Why'd you do it? Ignore Pretty Leslie that way? Ask me to get ice cream?"

He's eating his water ice really slowly and still has half of it left in his cup. "I know what it's like to have secrets, or rather, private things. Family shouldn't be tossed around that way to try and bag some dude. Plus, I wanted to get to know you better. I know we aren't friends . . . but maybe we can become friends."

I pretend to flick him in the face and he spills some of his water ice trying to back away.

He points at me. "Cheap shot, Santi,

149

cheap shot." He wipes off his jacket with the napkin I hand him. "You're not going to ask me what it is?"

I raise an eyebrow.

"The secret about my family."

I shrug. "If you wanted me to know something you'd tell me yourself."

"So you didn't want me to know about your daughter?"

I spread my hands wide, an open book. "Malachi, I was pregnant most of my freshman year. Everyone knows. It's not some big secret. But speaking of my daughter, I need to get home. Thank you for inviting me to kick it."

Malachi and I turn our backs to the river and he stands on the outside of the street, protecting me from cars as we walk to the train station. I keep a tight leash on the words that yank on my tongue: *I want to get to know you, too.*

PHONE CALLS

I convince Malachi we only need to ride the train together, but he doesn't have to get off, since he lives several stops after mine and it doesn't make sense for him to get off only to hop back on. I can tell he wants to fight me on it, but we both know it makes no sense for him to be riding the train for an extra hour.

The smile he put on my face is still clinging onto my lips when I walk through the house door. " 'Buela! I'm home."

She rushes to meet me and at the sight of her wrinkled forehead, my smile loses its grip and falls off my face.

" 'Buela, what's wrong? Babygirl?" I make a move for the couch, but she blocks me with her body.

"Where were you? I expected you home half an hour ago. I've been calling you and it was going straight to voice mail," she says. I take a breath. Whatever's wrong can't be that bad if she still has it in her to nag.

I drop my book bag. "I'm sorry. I went to get water ice with Angelica and a friend, and you know how the reception on my phone is when I'm on the train. I just lost track of time."

"Yes, you did. Why didn't you text me? I needed to leave for a doctor's appointment fifteen minutes ago."

"Another one? Is your hand acting up?" This is the second one this month. 'Buela had a lot of doctor visits when she got injured at work years ago, but never this many so often. 'Buela worked at the Macy's on Walnut Street before it was even a Macy's, back when it was a Wanamaker's. She was a seamstress in the alterations department. She worked there for over thirty years, through several store transitions, from the first week she got to

Philadelphia until the day she was injured on the job. The fingers on her right hand got caught in a machine, and even after surgery her hand was never really the same. I was still in elementary school and no one was there to pick me up. All the other kids had left before Ms. Martinez, our next-door neighbor, came to get me, explaining that 'Buela had been taken in an ambulance to the hospital. I was scared shitless then, because my whole life I've heard 'Buela say ambulances are too expensive and she'd rather catch a cab than ever call one, so I knew whatever had happened to her was serious.

When 'Buela finally called from the hospital she tried to sound normal and play it off as no big deal, even though her injury was serious enough that she came home with her hand bandaged and her fingers stitched, and she never worked in an official capacity as a seamstress again. And now my mind wants to jump to worst-case scenarios: her hand is giving her pain; she's sick, really sick, and she doesn't want to tell me. I'm scared of her answer. It's probably selfish, but the first thought I have is: What would I do without 'Buela? She's the starch in my spine, the only hand here to unfurl the wrinkles from my brows, the arms that hold me when I feel like I'm collapsing. I can't imagine a life without her. My thoughts must show on my face.

"I'm fine, m'ija. It's just a quick visit, a follow-up. Nothing to worry about." She pats my arm. "I got worried because you were late, and Julio called. You know how my nerves get when I speak to him."

I want to ask more questions about her doctor's appointment, but the mention of Julio puts a pause on that conversation. My father is an activist, a big community organizer who holds monthly meetings and lectures at his barbershop in San Juan, so he's often busy and yet he's called twice in the last two weeks. But after how he left this summer, I've been avoiding him.

She drops her arm and I walk into the living room where Babygirl is bouncing along with some Bubble Guppies on TV. I still feel shaken up by 'Buela jumping down my throat with the news that she has another doctor's appointment, and that Julio called again.

"You got to call your father back, nena. You know how he gets when you're slow to return his call."

"But he didn't call me, he called you." I bite my tongue when I hear the whine in my voice, but 'Buela doesn't let it drop.

"Don't start with that tone, Emoni. He calls me because he's my child. And he asked for you to call him. Now you call him because you're his child."

I drop into a squat in front of my own kid. "Hey, Babygirl! Come give Mommy a hug. Don't worry, when you grow up I'll call you and you'll call me and no one will summon anyone like they're king of the world." I keep my voice light and happy, holding out my arms to her. She quickly reaches for me.

My father isn't a bad man. He helps a lot of people. He keeps kids' books in his barbershop to help encourage the children in the community to read. He's constantly bringing in public speakers to discuss Puerto Rican rights and community concerns, and around the time I got pregnant with Babygirl he began a food drive to help single mothers. But his passions confuse me. Although he raises money for his causes, he never sends any here. Although he cares about his community, his own family gets the short end of the stick. It's like the best of him is reserved for strangers. And it mixes me up, like batter that isn't fully blended so there are still hard lumps baking beneath the surface.

I force myself to take a deep breath. Babygirl smells like baby and soap, but her face smells slightly of old milk. I grab a wipe from her baby bag and clean her cheek. I let go of her so she can keep dancing. My hands fidget with the throw pillows and the plastic of the sofa cover as I try to get my emotions under control. I look to the living room doorway, where 'Buela stands with her arms crossed.

Thinking about Julio makes my skin itchy. He makes me want to scream; he makes my throat feel clogged. I love my father, but I also might be allergic to him.

I don't say anything to 'Buela, and after a long moment she grabs her purse from the coatrack by the door. "Baby Emma had a small snack, but she'll probably be hungry soon. Don't worry about saving me dinner. I'll pick up something after my appointment. Te quiero, nena."

"Te quiero también, 'Buela," I whisper to the closed door.

Julio, Oh, Julio

"Hola, Emoni. How are you? About time you called your father."

I know I've caught Julio at his shop. I can hear razors buzzing and the background noise of grown men murmuring. I can picture him, head cocked to the side so he can press his phone to his ear with his shoulder, his long locs in a ponytail down his back as he creates a perfect right angle out of a customer's hairline.

"I'm good, Julio. How are you?"

Buzz, buzz, buzz. "You know I'm always good. Aquí, busy, busy. Your grandmother tells me you are taking a cooking class in school. And you are going to Spain. That true?"

'Buela. She harasses me into calling my father but has already given him a full update. "Only if I can afford it."

"Mm-hmm. And why Spain? They wanted you to learn how to cook some real food, they should have brought you here."

My father is big fan of the island. And he is not a big fan of Europe. He has a lot of ideas about the way they treated Latin America and the Caribbean when they were in power and believes they (and the United States) are the sole reason why so many of those countries are struggling now. And in case I forget how he feels, he never hesitates to launch into one of his history lessons. "You know that just because they were un poder colonial doesn't mean they are the center of the world, right, Emoni? What have I always told you? Be proud of who you are so you don't have to imitate or bow down to your oppressor."

Oh man. Julio's clippers have turned off, which lets me know if I don't jump in right now I'll be on the phone for an hour hearing a rant on how we are taught to idolize international superpowers. "Julio, I don't think we are going to Spain because they were once a colonial power. I think it's because my instructor really loves Spanish cuisine."

"Pftt. Everything they know how to make over there, they learned over here."

Probably not everything. I'm sure there *has* been an exchange of cuisine back and forth, especially with spices, but I doubt *every* dish was made in Puerto Rico first. Most of my father's beliefs are based on hard facts that every now and then are seasoned with hyperbole.

He must tell I'm not going to answer him because after a moment he changes the subject. "How's my little love doing?"

I describe Babygirl's daycare, and the new words she's learning. He summarizes the biography on Roberto Clemente he read recently. By the time he tells me he needs to get off the phone, I'm sure he's cut two heads, and has started on a third. But still, when we hang up, neither one of us says I love you. Neither one of us says I miss you. Neither one of says just come live here, with me. He doesn't say, I'm sorry for leaving. And I don't say, I'm so angry you left.

SCHOOL

"All right, folks. I know that we've been talking about where you're applying, and I'll be circling around to conference with each of you on your selections. While you're waiting, go ahead and fill out the survey in front of you with different majors, job opportunities, and fields to consider."

I give a head-nod to Malachi, who walks in late. Before we went our separate ways on the train, he saved his number on my phone. I texted him after I spoke with Julio and let him know I got in okay, but he didn't respond until an hour later, and by then I was making dinner, then bathing Babygirl before bed, and then sliding straight into my homework. I never did manage to text him back. The water-ice date was nice, but 'Buela's reaction to my being out so long was a reminder I don't have time to waste chopping it up and flirting with boys.

I stare at Ms. Fuentes's questionnaire, filling in answers about my temperament, ideal work schedule, desired income, and experience. I'm on the third page when Ms. Fuentes sits down at the empty desk next to me.

"Hey, Ms. Santiago. What are you thinking?"

I shrug. "I know we've talked about it a little, but the guidance counselor says my grades 'leave a lot to be desired.' She thinks the majority of schools in the city I was looking into might be a reach. I'm wondering if it makes more sense to get a good job after high school and focus on that instead of this application."

"Because of Emma?"

I hesitate for a second, because saying Babygirl is the reason would be easier. But I don't know if it's the whole truth. "I can't ask my grandmother to take care of Babygirl forever. I don't *want* my grandmother to do that. I want to be able to take care of my own, and the only thing I would want to study is culinary arts, but why try to learn that in a school when I could learn it in a real restaurant where I'm making money instead of spending it?"

I can tell that Ms. Fuentes doesn't like that answer. She frowns so hard her brows meet in the middle. "Don't you think it'll be better in the long run for your family if you have a college degree? Then if cooking doesn't work out, you have other options. I just want you to make something of yourself," Ms. Fuentes says.

I almost suck my teeth. I love Ms. Fuentes, but sometimes she says real stupid shit. "I think there are lots of ways to 'make something' of yourself and still support your family. College isn't the only way."

She nods. "Of course. I'm sorry if what I said came across wrong; I just want you to apply to college so, come April, at least you have the option of deciding to do something else. At least then you'll have choices. And who knows? Your mind-set about school might change in a few months."

I look at Ms. Fuentes. She's young, maybe early thirties, not like a lot of the teachers at the school. And she's hip to most things like fashion and music, but she doesn't have a kid. She doesn't have a grandmother who's spent the last thirty-five years raising a son and then her son's kid and now her son's kid's kid. No, Ms. Fuentes has a job that she seems to like, and she can afford nice perfume, and cute outfits, and pretty manicures, and to give out advice nobody asked for.

I don't tell Ms. Fuentes that I just don't think more school is for me. That I'd rather save my money for my daughter's college tuition instead of my own. That when I think of my hopes and dreams I don't think I can follow them from a classroom. That my hopes and dreams seem so far out of reach I have to squint to see them, so how could I possibly pursue them?

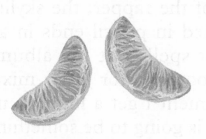

GOING PLACES

"Angelica, this is amazing." I look at the mock-up album cover she created for a rapper who graduated last year. He has a mixtape coming out in a month and everybody who's gone to Schomburg knows if you need artwork done for a project, Angelica is your girl. She's had this side hustle for years and it's one of the ways she's able to keep herself dressed like she's in her own reality TV show. Angelica has her peanut-butter sandwich halfway to her mouth.

"You like it? It was something light. He didn't have much of a budget to work with."

I shake my head. Angelica's "something light" is something most people would frame. The cover shows a hand-drawn version of the rapper; the skyline behind him etched in pencil ends in an elegant loop that spells out the album's name. This is too good for just a mixtape. And for a moment I get a lump in my throat. Angelica is going to be something big one day. She's going to be the go-to person for famous people's art. And I'm so, so hype for her. And I'm also going to still be here, left behind.

I force myself to smile.

"If you don't get a full scholarship, I'll fight the admissions officers myself. Your portfolio must be a hundred times better than other applicants'."

She shrugs and takes a bite of her sandwich. "Let's hope so, girl."

I mix soy sauce, ketchup, and a packet of sugar and try and make a mock Korean BBQ sauce for my chicken nuggets.

Angelica puts her hand on mine. "Stop playing with your food, Emoni. You only play with your food when you're upset. What's wrong?"

And now it's my turn to shrug. "I guess it's a lot of things. My father called last night, and although we had a long conversation, I just don't know; I'm still mad at him. 'Buela has been having all these doctor appointments and she says it's nothing but I don't believe her; she won't meet my eyes when she says it. And I don't know what to do about college." I don't mention the mixed-up feelings I've been having about Malachi.

"Mmm, you got a lot going on. I hope Abuela Gloria is okay. Maybe her doctor's appointments are just checkups or something? What was Ms. Fuentes saying about college? Mr. Goldberg was going on and on about the college applications and how we're going to have to start turning those in. Jesus, it's not even November yet."

"Yeah, but it's the middle of October next week. And before you know it it'll be December, when everything is due to the guidance counselor for review," I say. The deadlines are all engraved into my mental calendar; I just don't know what I'm going to do about them.

"What are you going to be for Halloween?" Angelica asks, finishing off her sandwich.

"Huh?" I laugh. She's always been that

way. Able to jump around from subject to subject and know exactly when to switch it up on me. But I know that she's also trying to take my mind off problems that I can't fix and she can't either. "What day of the week is it this year?"

"A Thursday," Angelica says, checking her phone calendar.

I shake my head. "I usually work Thursdays. But maybe I need to start thinking about what I'll dress Babygirl as in case 'Buela wants to take her out."

Angelica's eyes widen and I glance around to see what she's looking at. "We should make her a costume! It'll be so cute."

I laugh again and eat another chicken nugget as Angelica sketches costumes on a napkin. The laughter helps ease the weight on my chest. And the sauce tastes just a little bit sweeter.

BASURA

The next day, I set my plate in front of Chef Ayden and he turns it round and round. I wait for him to pick up his fork and knife.

"Trash it," he says without looking up at me.

"Ex-excuse me?" I stutter out. Is he kidding? I look around the room but none of the other students meets my eyes. They are all standing, waiting to present their dishes, but our usually noisy class is suddenly very quiet. Malachi is the only person not pretending he's not all in my business, and his eyebrows quirk in confusion, as if he's stuck on Chef's command as well.

"Trash it," Chef says again, but this

time he looks at me straight on.

"What's wrong with it?" I ask. I know the twitch in my jaw is probably showing. I can't believe he would tell me to throw away something he hasn't even tasted!

"It's not the recipe I gave you. It doesn't have the same ingredients, and the cut on these is wrong."

"It tastes good, it's well-balanced like you tell us to do, and the presentation is flawless," I say through my teeth.

He grabs a fork, stabs the dish, and pops it in his mouth. He's quiet for a long moment. And I can tell he *loves* it. He shakes his head. "Cumin, basil, oregano." His eyes pop open. "None of those ingredients were in the recipe. This isn't the same dish at all. I can't grade something that is more about creativity than execution. That wasn't the point of today's evaluation. So I won't say it again: trash it." He sets his fork down.

My eyes sting but I bite my lip hard and grab my dish. I slap the plastic plate against the side of the trash bin and the food slides off. With my hands shaking, I unbutton my chef's jacket, tug off my scarf. When the bell rings, I wait for everyone else to leave. Malachi is the last student left besides me and he touches my arm on his way to the door. "Come with me, Santi. Let this one go."

I shake his hand off.

Chef is behind his long metal table entering the last of the grades in his laptop. He lifts his head slowly. "Yes, Emoni. Can I help you with something?"

I know my anger is like graffiti tagged onto my face and I don't care if he can see. "Why'd you make me do that?"

Almost as if in response to the bite in my voice, his voice gets even calmer. "You didn't prepare the dish correctly."

"So what? It tasted good."

"I told you before, sometimes following directions isn't about stifling your creativity, it's about showing respect. You have a complete disregard for the rules. That's all well and good, when you're a professional. But when you're learning, you need to know the rules before you break them."

"That doesn't make sense. What if the rules are stupid? What if that wasn't a great recipe to begin with? Why should I learn to make a bad recipe well?"

He shakes his head. "It's not about my rules, Emoni. Or my recipes. A customer walks in and asks for a flank steak, medium rare. At what internal temperature do you pull the steak off the grill?"

I pause and think.

"It's burning, Emoni. The steak is burning because you can't remember the temperature or timing and now the customer is upset that it's too tough and they won't be coming back. And it was only a small, technical rule. What if a customer is allergic to cayenne, and it doesn't say that's in the ingredient list, but you wanted to *express yourself* at the last minute and now the customer is sick. I could come up with a hundred scenarios."

He holds my gaze one second longer, then goes back to his laptop. He doesn't have to say that I've been dismissed for me to know it.

I slam his door behind me, knowing exactly how much it annoys Chef when students do that. It doesn't matter. After

today, I don't think I'll be his student
much longer.

HOME IS WHERE

I cut last-period English for the first time since I was a freshman. I spent some time out of school while I was pregnant, so I've tried to be really aware of the absences I rack up. But with only one class left, and my hands still trembling after Culinary Arts, I can't sit in a classroom trying to talk about how Baldwin depicts religion and race in his work.

The security guard should probably stop me, but with so many seniors constantly leaving the building for doctor appointments and interviews, or because they are done for the day, the guard on duty hardly glances my way before waving me on.

And so, I go to the only person who

174

can make me feel better.

Babygirl's daycare isn't too far from the house, and instead of taking the bus or train, I walk the whole way there, using the hour to clear my head and getting there right around pickup time. I peek through the window into her classroom. She's standing at a play kitchen swinging a large plastic spoon. It's one of the cutest things I've ever seen and for some reason I tear up. I don't stop looking even when I smell the soft scent of vanilla.

"Doesn't it just fill your heart up?" 'Buela asks me. I should have texted her to tell her I'd pick up Babygirl today.

I nod. I don't need to answer that. She can probably see it on my face.

"Aren't you going to ask me why I'm not in school?" I finally say.

'Buela is still looking at Babygirl through the window. "In a couple of months you'll be an adult. I trust you with that child; I should trust you with yourself."

And although her trust should make me feel better, I feel a slight pang in my chest. Every day it seems 'Buela is stepping back, not just giving me full rein in Babygirl's life, but also in my own. And I know I should love the freedom, but I don't think I'm ready for all the safety nets to be cut loose. Doesn't she know I still need her? That I still wish someone would look at the pieces of my life and tell me how to make sure they all fit back together?

I Been Grown

Here's the thing: These teachers forget that I have to make hard decisions every day. That I've been doing that for almost three years and that I know when they are trying to convince me to do something *they* think is right without them knowing my situation. I've had to decide whether it was better to breastfeed or wean Babygirl early so I wasn't dripping milk in class. Whether I should tell my father how I feel about his absence or suck it up and be thankful that at least I have a father. Whether it's safe to send my daughter to a daycare I don't know, or try to coax 'Buela to raise a toddler when she's tired and has other obligations.

Whether I should have had a baby.

And that was probably the hardest decision I've ever made. No one had the right answers; no one knew if I could cut it as a mom or if I should give the baby up for adoption. If I should have aborted her. For all his faults, Tyrone never pushed me in any direction. His parents wanted the baby gone, but Tyrone told me I should decide. 'Buela cried the night I told her I was pregnant, big, silent sobs, and I know it was partly for me and partly for her — she'd thought she'd raised her last child.

"Emoni, pregúntate, are you ready? If you have this baby, your life will no longer be about you. Every decision you make will have to include this child. You can't be selfish anymore; you can't put your wants above the baby's. This is the last time someone will ask you what *you* want before asking you what your baby needs. Piénsalo bien."

'Buela is a soft Catholic. She believes in the teachings of God, but she doesn't push her religion on people. I went to church with her on Sundays, but she didn't force me to do communion or confirmation. And she didn't force me to keep the baby. She just held my hand and told me to think about what it would mean. I was fourteen; I had no idea what it would mean.

Julio was silent when I told him over the phone. Finally he asked me to put 'Buela on, and she took the phone into her room. We never talked about my pregnancy again. He didn't ask if I would keep the baby or not.

Without telling anyone, I went to the free clinic. I sat in the plastic chair. I didn't have a big belly yet, no swollen feet, no one kicking inside me reminding me of their presence. I didn't have anything but a pee test and a missed period as evidence of a baby. The nurses at the clinic were so nice. The doctor treated me like a full adult and told me all the options, all the risks, all the procedures. She didn't push anything on me, and she also didn't pity me.

And the only question I kept asking myself was, "Can I do this?" And I re-

alized there wasn't going to be a perfect
answer, only the right answer for me.

Hurricane Season

'Buela is watching the news before the Sunday-night game begins while I study for my ServSafe quiz this week. Babygirl should be back in about an hour and I can't wait to hold her. All weekend Tyrone sent me pictures of her and updates, and it feels like we are finally falling into a rhythm during these visits.

At 'Buela's soft gasp I look up at the TV, expecting to see that one of her favorite players was injured. But instead it's the weather forecast, and at the image of swirling clouds in the south my chest tightens. 'Buela and I both know what storms mean for North Carolina and especially Puerto Rico. It wasn't that long ago that a hurricane hit the island and caused more destruction than we'd ever seen.

That last time we didn't hear from Julio for more than three weeks.

'Buela could barely eat, and I only slept a handful of hours a night. We would just keep trying his cell phone and contacting hotlines to see if anyone had heard from him. But there was no news. I spent days trying to track down people in his neighborhood only to be told no one had seen him. I was more afraid during those weeks than I'd been even while in labor. And I was pretty scared then, being that my mother didn't make it out of labor alive. But the fear you have for someone else's life always eclipses the fear you have for your own.

And now when folks have barely gotten on their feet it seems like another storm is coming.

"Did you return your father's last call?"

I nod. And thank goodness I called him this past Wednesday even though that phone call was tense. I take my hurt feelings and fold them small, tucking them away in a corner of my heart. Right now, they don't matter.

"Emoni! Twice in one week, it must be my birthday."

I'm already speaking before he finishes his sentence. "Julio, there's a storm forming near you. Did you see? It's supposed to make landfall in a week."

And I wait for him to shrug it off like he usually does whenever there's a storm. He's always so quick to say that nothing and no one will make him leave his island, but there's a slight pause after my question as if Julio is trying to find the words to say to me. "I saw, of course I saw, Emoni. We are storing provisions at the shop and making sure generators are up and running in case power gives out. The barrio has a plan and I'm seeing to it folks are safe."

And then we are both quiet, because I don't know how to tell him I think he should get out of harm's way. And I don't think he knows how to say those words, either.

'Buela saves us both. "Ask Julio if he's coming here. We need to get him a flight. They're saying this storm is going to be bad."

He must hear her through the phone because he answers before I repeat the question. "Tell Mami I'm not leaving my

183

home. This is where I was born. This is where I live. This is where I'll die, whenever God decides that should be. You gotta make your home better; you don't just run because you can. The community needs as many people organizing as possible."

I nod into the phone even though he can't see me. And we sit still like that for a while, listening to each other breathe.

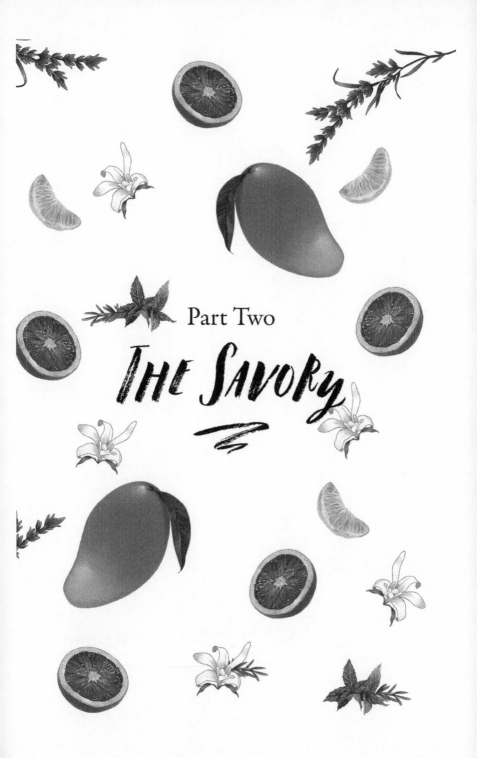

Part Two

THE SAVORY

EMONI'S RECIPE
"NO USE CRYING OVER SPILLED STRAWBERRY MILK"

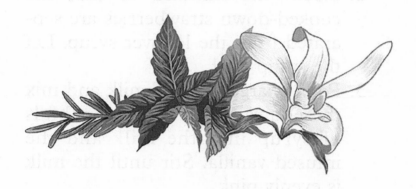

*Serves: Your ego when you're
full of regret.*

Ingredients:

As many strawberries as you can find
Sugar to taste
Enough water to cover the sugar
A glass and a half of whole milk
Three drops of Caribbean vanilla extract
  infused with mint

Directions:

1. In a saucepan, heat strawberries,
   water, and sugar until it boils.
   Water will begin to evaporate and
   the mixture will thicken until it

looks like jam. Keep on the stove for the duration of three listens to a Cardi B song.

2. Strain the mixture so that the cooked-down strawberries are separated from the leftover syrup. Let the syrup cool.

3. Pour a large glass of milk and mix the equivalent of three mouthfuls of syrup into the milk and the infused vanilla. Stir until the milk is evenly pink.

*Best enjoyed while playing hide-and-seek with your toddler and listening to Rihanna's top hits.

SKIPPING

I don't go to Culinary Arts the following Monday. I sneak into the library through the back entrance instead. The library is nice and quiet and teachers rarely look for students here.

When Wednesday afternoon rolls around, I still don't go to class. Malachi somehow sneaks off a text asking me where I am. I send him a smiley-face emoji but nothing else. He shoots me questioning looks during Advisory every morning, but I shake my head, and he finally stops asking me about class and we talk about other things. I spend the whole week doing assignments in the library and ignoring the absences I'm racking up. At some point Ms. Fuentes will receive a notice letting her know one of her students isn't attending a class.

And I know that I'm also setting myself up to fail the class. But although I never want to go back to Culinary Arts, I also can't bring myself to drop it completely, and it doesn't seem ready to drop me, either; in fact, it confronts me at the Burger Joint.

Ding. Ding. Ding.

I move to the assembly line and grab the order of burgers and fries, juggling them on the tray before handing them to my customer. She wishes me a nice day and moves off, and the next customer moves forward. I pull my visor tight around my ponytail and look up.

Malachi. It's Friday afternoon and I've missed an entire week of Culinary Arts classes. I've also only responded to his texts with one-word answers and emojis. He keeps asking me if I'm coming back to class, and if I'm okay, and honestly, I don't know the answer to either of those questions, so it's easier to keep it light and simple with memes and song lyrics.

But now, Malachi is here, in the Burger Joint, with Pretty Leslie next to him. If he's surprised to see me he doesn't let on, but she smiles, her red-painted lips like a curtain parting above her teeth. And I can almost imagine her greeting me in a circus conductor's voice. *Ta-da! Here's me taking another shot at embarrassing you, bitch!*

"Emoni," she says, like we're old friends, making the last syllable last three seconds. "Hey, giiirl." She bats her long fake lashes at me and I want to pluck each one from her face.

"Welcome to the Burger Joint. Can I take your order?" I ask them with the same tone I use for every customer. I know I owe Malachi more than this, but I just don't have the energy to pretend to be nice to Pretty Leslie or to wonder why he's here with her at all.

"I'll have a number two, extra cheese, the pickle on the side, the fries extra crisp, and barbecue sauce. Oh, and one of those apple-pie pockets. They're so good . . . maybe I should get ice cream to go with it." Pretty Leslie taps a long red nail against her chin. It matches the color of her lip stain exactly. I click in the order and wait for her to decide. I can't tell if the ice-cream thing is real or if she's trying to allude to Malachi's and my ice-cream date. "No, no ice cream. I have more than enough without it."

I raise an eyebrow at Malachi but don't say anything.

"I'll have a number five, with a cup of tap water."

I punch his order in. "Together or separate?"

Pretty Leslie giggles. "Together. Oh, Emoni. It must be so nice to work with food even though you quit our class. I'm sure you learn a lot here."

Malachi raises an eyebrow at her and moves toward the far wall but she doesn't budge.

I smile at Pretty Leslie. "I appreciate your concern. When your order is ready it will be handed to you over there." I point to the receiving counter.

She walks away, making sure I see the smirk on her face.

"Emoni, stop fraternizing with the customers. Even if they are your friends from school," Steve says from behind me. I sigh and look at the next customer.

"Welcome to the Burger Joint. Can I take your order?"

FORGIVENESS

'Buela is watching TV on the couch when I get home. I drop my book bag on the coatrack, kiss her forehead, and walk into my room, where Babygirl is already asleep in her crib. Recently she's been pulling herself halfway over the railing and I know she'll be climbing in and out soon. I scan the space. I don't know how we're going to fit another bed in here, but we are going to have to figure it out sometime down the line. Maybe I can angle mine and have a cool diagonal room setup. I rub her dark hair from her forehead before placing a kiss on each eyebrow.

It's technically Tyrone's weekend, but

he and his and family are traveling to a funeral and I didn't feel comfortable with them taking Babygirl, so we switched this weekend's visit to next week. I'm so glad she'll be home with me.

When I go back into the living room 'Buela pats the seat of the couch beside her.

"How was your day, nena?"

"Long. The bus was running late, or I would have been home in time to put her to bed. Thank you for doing that. Was she good?"

"She was fine."

I nod and close my eyes.

"Your father called." She puts a hand up before I can say anything. "He's fine. It had nothing to do with the storm. He was asking for you to call him. I know, he can just call you on your cell phone. I told him that, but he says you're the child, et cetera."

I laugh and open my eyes. "That man is hilarious. Who does he think he is?"

'Buela raises an eyebrow. "Your father. And you know his brain's scattered dealing with the coming storm."

I nod. 'Buela and I do not see eye to eye when it comes to my father, but I know in this moment she's right. "Emoni, yo sé, you have a lot of hard feelings about him. You can't hold that anger inside."

"I'll give him a call later and make sure he doesn't need anything."

But when I grab my phone it's to call Angelica.

"Hey, Gelly, I'm going shopping in the morning for the groceries. This is your last chance to change the menu." I've had her dinner all planned out for weeks and tomorrow I get to put those plans together. Gelly left the money I need to buy the supplies in our locker, and what I have planned for her is better than even she could imagine.

"I don't want to change anything. Just make sure it's fancy. Something you're learning about in class."

I haven't told her yet. I haven't told her or 'Buela that I've stopped going to class.

"I got you."

"Great. I've already started planning

Babygirl's Halloween costume, so it'll be even."

"Angelica, we'll always be even in my book. No owing here."

And I don't have to see her smile to know it's there.

SISTERHOOD

When the baby bump began to show, the kids at school and around the way began to talk shit. (I know I'm supposed to be working on my cursing, but there's really no other way to put it.) We'd had pregnant girls in school before, but it was like I was something brand-new. Maybe because I was young and petite, yet by the end of freshman year I looked like a basketball was trying to set itself free from inside my belly. Maybe because people thought I was conceited since I mostly kept to myself. Maybe because even though Tyrone didn't go to our school, most of the girls at Schomburg Charter knew him or had heard about him and no one could really figure out why he'd chosen to get with me.

The snide comments and behind-my-back chatter was happening before Angelica came out, when all the guys on the football team were trying to bag her and the girls all wanted her to sit with them at lunch. I waited for her to start talking mess, too, because it's just the way things seemed to go even if we'd been friends forever. But if we'd been close before, we became even closer then. Angelica? She shut that mess all the way down. Anytime she heard a whisper of someone talking about me she was in their face. If a guy made a comment about me being a ho she cursed him out and never spoke to him again.

When she told me she was a lesbian, I asked her if she'd had a crush on me. If that was why she'd been so hell-bent on defending me.

"Ew, no," she'd said, her face twisted as if she'd smelled week-old milk. "That'd be like incest or something. Do you have a crush on everyone you're friends with or defend?"

I learned a lot about what it meant to be a fierce friend, to protect someone and learn more about what it was like to walk in their shoes. When she did come out junior year, I held her down like she did me. Walked beside her when people talked behind their hands. Made sure to get to our locker every day before she did and pull off any ugly Post-its kids had taped there.

And when people had the balls to ask us if we were girlfriends, I held her hand tight, the way she'd held mine when I was pregnant and scared, and we walked down the halls together. And folks learned quick, if they had a problem with Angelica, they could mix me. If they had a problem with me, they were facing two of us.

And ain't that what it means to be a sister? Holding things tight when the other one is falling apart?

INVITATIONS

"Hello, Santi?" I raise an eyebrow and stare at my cell phone. I don't usually answer unknown numbers, but I was so busy organizing the groceries for Angelica's dinner I answered without thinking.

"Malachi?"

The laugh he gives after isn't his usual suave one and I wonder if he's nervous. For some reason I feel myself soften at the thought of Malachi anxiously dialing my number.

I glance around the kitchen, knowing it's the most private place in the apartment unless I want to hide in the bathroom. I pull out the small chair from the corner table and sit. "What number are you calling me from?"

"It's the house phone at my aunt's. My cell is acting up and I wanted to speak to you."

Oh. I wonder if I would have picked up if I'd known it was Malachi. I picture how he looked at the Burger Joint when Pretty Leslie kept putting me on the spot. "Wassup, Malachi?"

There's a long pause on the other end of the phone. "I just wanted to apologize for yesterday. For Leslie. She was out of line. I never meant to make you uncomfortable."

"Not a problem. I don't feel uncomfortable for working, at a food spot or otherwise. I've had a lot of things to feel ashamed about and I've learned most of them are other people's problems, not mine."

We're both quiet for a moment. I hadn't meant to say that. For some reason, I always say more than I need to whenever Malachi is the one listening.

He clears his throat. "I was hoping I could see you. That we could talk?"

"What, Pretty Leslie is busy?" As soon as I say it, I wish I could bite my tongue.

It's not my business what he does with Pretty Leslie. I shouldn't have even mentioned her at all. See? My mouth out here sprinting across every yard line and thinking it runs itself.

Malachi is quiet a long moment. And when he speaks, he sounds like his familiar self for the first time during this conversation. "What, you jealous? I thought we weren't even friends."

"Nope, I shouldn't have said anything. Just don't want you feeling like you're out here juggling girls. If you are trying to get with her, I hope you aren't trying to get with me."

"I don't feel that way at all. I'm not trying to juggle anyone. I don't know why Leslie acts the way she does around you, but she's different with me. She's my friend. That's all."

I shake my head. Dudes can be real oblivious sometimes. "That might be all it is for you, but trust me, I've known about Pretty Leslie since middle school. She isn't nice to people for the sake of it. She likes you."

Malachi sighs. "And I like her. As a friend. She's gone through a lot in her life and I think we relate to one another, but I'm not trying to get with her like that. So, can I? Kick it with you, I mean."

There's a lot more I want to ask about his relationship with Pretty Leslie. *Has* she gone through a lot? Every time I see her she's pouting and flipping her bangs, and seems like the only care she has is what nail color she should wear next. But against my better judgment I reply, "I'm home with my daughter and grand-mother all day. Cooking for an event this evening."

"Maybe I can come by and help? Every-one needs a sous chef sometimes, right, Chef Santi?"

SOUS CHEF

"So, este Malachi from school, what do you know about him?" 'Buela asks. She's at the kitchen sink washing the dishes from lunch as I feed Babygirl the last of her food. And by feed, I mean I'm trying to get her to stop playing with the rice kernels in her bowl and actually get them into her mouth, where I hope some of them will get swallowed instead of just spit back out into a spittle mosaic on her plate.

"I know he lives in Oxford Circle with his aunt. And he's originally from New Jersey. He's a senior like me and transferred in last month. I know that he has a sense of humor."

"Is he kind?" 'Buela turns the water off

and dries the last of the dishes before folding the towel over the sink.

Babygirl dodges another spoonful of food. "Yeah, he is kind. Very polite."

She nods. "So, you're dating?"

I almost drop the spoon. "No, 'Buela! Jesus, we're just friends. Not even that. Just classmates. When have you known me to date anyone since Tyrone?"

'Buela has her back to me but she's completely still. "Okay. I just think Baby Emma's a little young for you to start bringing more boys around."

I put the spoon down. Even after what I told Malachi about shame, 'Buela's words land like a slap. I swallow and keep my voice soft and neutral when I say, "I'm not 'bringing more boys around.' He's just going to help me make this meal for Angelica and Laura. I don't even know if I'm introducing him to Baby-girl."

'Buela nods and hands me a napkin. I wipe rice from Babygirl's chin.

■ ■ ■ ■

"So have you made this before?" Malachi asks as he pulls the pot of pasta off the fire.

I almost called and told him not to come. After the talk with 'Buela, I realized this could become more drama than it's worth. But by then he was probably already on his way and it didn't make sense. Or maybe I still wanted him to come through. All I know is that he's here.

"Nope. It's my aunt's recipe, but I'm going to give it something extra."

"You always do; that's probably why Chef Ayden gets so angry."

I shrug. "He won't have to be angry anymore. He has all the little soldiers he needs." I give him a two-finger salute.

He shakes his head and opens the fridge to place the butter back. I add the last of the seasonings on the filet and turn to get a large skillet. 'Buela walks to the doorway. She's been watching Baby-girl in her room; I'd decided not to introduce her to Malachi after all.

"So, Malachi. You like the cooking class you take with Emoni?" 'Buela asks.

I shoot him a look and he raises an eyebrow at me, but when he turns to 'Buela he's all dimples. I don't know how good he is at silent communication but I need him to keep his mouth shut about the class. No pudding jokes. No three-some jokes. No "trash it" jokes. And most definitely not the truth: that I haven't been going to class.

"Mrs. Santiago, I really do like the class. I did a lot of the cooking growing up because my mother worked late and I was the oldest. So I was the one making sure my brother was well fed."

I look at him, surprised. I didn't know he grew up cooking, or anything about his family, really. 'Buela blinks slowly, the way she does when she's translating fast English into Spanish. "You were the oldest but not anymore?"

Malachi straightens and shakes his head, his smile falling off his face. He pauses for a long moment as if having an internal debate. The gentle look on 'Buela's face must decide it for him.

"My little brother was killed last February. Some beef in the neighborhood back home and he was shot. It's unclear if it was a stray bullet or meant for him." He doesn't look at me as he speaks. Keeps his eyes steady on 'Buela's. I tighten my hands on the kitchen counter. My heart squeezes in my chest. "My moms didn't want me caught up in the same drama so she sent me down here to live with my aunt even though it's less than two hours away. But Moms says the block would eat me up and spit me out and she couldn't watch that happen again. Now there's no reason for me to cook anymore since Aunt Brenda works regular hours and gets dinner on the table without me." I don't know if a shrug can be a sad thing or not, but that small movement of his shoulders knots something in my throat.

The oven timer goes off but I ignore it. Out of my control, my hand halfway reaches out to touch Malachi's back but then I pull it to my side. I don't want anyone in the room getting the wrong impression. Myself included. But 'Buela does it for me. She walks to Malachi, who is double her size, and pulls him into a fierce hug. She pats his back with soft thumps that sound just like a heartbeat.

"It isn't easy to lose a family member. Thank you for sharing that with me. I'm glad you and Emoni are friends."

She pulls back from him while still holding his arms. Looks up into his eyes. "But take care it doesn't become more than that. I don't want to see either of you hurt."

'Buela has a way of letting you know she cares for you — and that she'll also beat that ass if you act up.

Malachi nods and then smiles. It's not his usual lightbulb smile but it gets close, and instantly 'Buela smiles back, pats his cheek. "You seem like a good boy. I won't get into that other one she brought here, since he helped make my granddaughter, but chacho, he wasn't an easy one to swallow. Don't let the pasta sit too long, Emoni; Angelica will kill you." She heads out of the kitchen toward the sound of cheering coming from her bedroom.

"Thanks for that," I say under my breath. I clear my throat. "Thanks for telling us that. For answering her questions. She's nosy." I move to the stove and turn the heat up. To get a nice sear on the steaks I'll need a hot pan and a quick hand before I finish the steak with the mac and cheese in the oven.

"Is your grandmother watching a football game?" Malachi asks from the doorway. Clearly he doesn't want to talk about his brother anymore.

"Oh, yeah. She's a huge Eagles fan, but since they don't play until tomorrow, she has to get her fix with college games."

Malachi's hand tickles the back of my neck and before I know it he pulls me in for a hug from behind. I stand with my hands stiffly by my sides, but when he doesn't let go, I lean against his forearm. And I wonder if he put cologne on the inside of his wrist, because he smells good.

"Emoni," he whispers into my hair.

"Mmm?" I ask. He's about to ruin this. He's going to try to kiss me or say something nasty. Boys are dumb like that. Always ruining the moment.

"I think you were wrong. We *are* friends. Your grandmother said so. And she seems like the kind of woman that knows what she's talking about. Even if she does have horrible taste in football teams."

I smile into his arm before bumping him away. I have a smoking skillet that needs my attention. And a correction to make. "The Eagles are definitely going to win the Super Bowl again this season. Just you watch."

ANNIVERSARY

Angelica opens the door wide, and Malachi and I maneuver our large bags full of plastic containers and décor into the living room. The house smells of Pine-Sol and incense and I know that Angelica cleaned even though the girl is mortal enemies with the broom. I didn't tell her Malachi was going to be with me; one of the things I've always loved about our friendship is how she didn't even blink an eye when she opened the door, but the moment Malachi begins unpacking the containers in the kitchen she raises an eyebrow and cocks her head in his direction. I shrug and give her a small smile. And although we don't say one word, we communicate everything that needs to be said.

Angelica clears her throat. "Malachi, I tried setting the table but I think I messed it all up." I peek into the living room where her small dining room table is. The utensils *are* in the wrong order and the water glass is on the left-hand side. Chef taught us in our second week how a proper table should be set. "Do you think you could fix it for me while Emoni shows me what to do with dinner? Laura gets here in twenty minutes and I know I need to preheat the oven or something."

"Yeah, I got you." Malachi walks to the little table and begins refolding the napkins and arranging the knives. Angelica grabs my hand and pulls me into the kitchen.

"What's he doing here? I thought he was dating Pretty Leslie?" Angelica says in a mock whisper. I guess not everything can be communicated with an eyebrow and a smile.

I put the oven on the correct setting and pull the lids off the sauces and individual portions of mac and cheese.

Aunt Sarah uses three cheeses, but I added an extra-stinky one to make it even creamier. I drew a diagram of exactly how Angelica needs to place the food onto the plate and where the sauces go so she can put everything together just in time for Laura. "I don't know. He called me today and wanted to chill. I figured it wouldn't hurt. It's not a date or anything and I needed the help to carry all this over."

Angelica gives me her "Yeah, whatever" look and opens the cabinet above the sink to pull down two white plates with vibrant green vines circling the edges.

"Will these work?" she asks. "They were my grandmother's plates and Mom and I only use them for Thanksgiving." The finger she traces along the engraved vines is shaking. I take the plates away from her and set them on the kitchen counter. I hold her hand in mine.

"Are you okay? You nervous about your mom finding out you had Laura here? I can come help you clean up tomorrow." Ms. Jackson is one of my favorite people in the world, and she and Angelica have a great relationship, but she doesn't care

214

how old Angelica is or what gender she's dating, she still runs a strict house when it comes to having people in it.

"It's not my mom. She knows Laura is coming over to have dinner."

I squeeze her hand. "What is it, boo?"

She shakes her head as if she isn't going to say anything, then she blurts out, "We haven't ever slept together."

I keep my reaction off of my face. Angelica is always so sure of herself, of her words, of her world. I don't recognize this girl who's biting the polish off a recently manicured nail. I grab that hand, too.

"Okay, and you all decided today you would?" I'm guessing here. Angelica doesn't usually bite her nails — or her tongue — but tonight she seems out of her element. She finally looks at me and nods.

"But the thing is, today is my first day. Ever. I mean I've kissed and fooled around with other girls but never more than that. What if I don't know what to do?"

I pull her smudged glasses off her face

and clean the lenses on my T-shirt. I can tell she needs a moment without me staring at her intensely. I slide them back onto the bridge of her nose.

"Angelica, now that you can see clearly, look at me. Laura loves you for you. She may have more experience in this arena, but I'm also sure she'll be fine with taking it slow and you'll figure it out together." I smile at her. She hadn't had these same butterflies when she had sex for the first time with a guy. She'd approached that with the full curiosity of a scientist even though it confirmed what she already knew about herself. But this is less about exploring, and more about expressing. I know how much this means to her.

I squeeze her hand. "You don't have to do anything you aren't comfortable doing. I'm sure Laura will understand."

She squeezes my hand back. "I know, I know. But I want to." Angelica smiles. "I'm just nervous as fuck."

I laugh. "You're going to be fine. I promise. I've put a little extra magic into my recipe so I can make that promise with full confidence. Now come look at

216

this picture I drew to show you how you're going to plate this food when Laura gets here."

Angelica takes one look at my drawing and busts out laughing. I watch her shoulders drop and her body shake as she laughs. "Emoni! That is the worst picture I've ever seen. I can't make out half these squiggles."

I press a hand to my heart and gasp. "How you going to play my art skills like that?"

Angelica takes out a pencil and redoes the diagram as I give her instructions. When she's done she gives me a small smile, and I can tell she's still nervous but ready for whatever the night might bring. "Thank you, Emoni."

I give her one last hug and then Malachi and I are out the door.

NETFLIX, NO CHILL

"That steak you put together was everything, Santi!" Malachi kisses his fingers like an old-school Chef Boyardee commercial. "They're going to love it, especially when she tries that mac and cheese." There was lightly massaged kale, too. But Malachi didn't try any of that.

"You want to know something crazy? I don't know if it was talking about my brother to your grandmother, but I had this memory that came out of nowhere. Of learning to make mac and cheese straight out the box. I think we spilled all that powdery orange sauce on ourselves and dropped the noodles on the floor, and when my moms came into the kitchen we had nothing to show for ourselves but boiling water and a mess." He laughs. And I reach over to squeeze his hand.

On the street outside of Angelica's house he grabs the bag of empty containers from me. I begin to protest but then shut my mouth. I have to say it's kind of nice to be able to stick my hands into my pockets and let someone else carry the dirty dishes for a change.

"I hope so. They deserve a nice dinner. They're a really cute couple." I face him. "Not sure what you have planned next. I need to get home and make sure Baby-girl and 'Buela are all right."

He gives me a nod and the dirty containers rattle inside the big bag 'Buela bought from the dollar store for groceries.

I look at him. Bite my lip. Pull out my phone. I click it on so the time projects brightly. Eight p.m. Still early. I slip the phone back into my pocket. "Do you want to come back? Watch TV or something? There were leftovers."

I expect him to smirk, or raise an eyebrow, but he just gives me a slow nod and keeps following me home. I've always been glad Gelly and I live close to each other, but never more than in this moment.

"I'm down to watch TV, but only if you promise we don't watch a scary movie. I hate scary movies." He pretends to shudder in fear, and the giggle that springs out my throat isn't something I've heard in a long time. It doesn't sound anything like me at all. I feel those first crush butterflies that I thought I'd never feel again, which I know sounds silly for a seventeen-year-old to say, but some days I don't feel like a seventeen-year-old at all.

"A big ole dude like you, scared of ghosts and masked killers?" I tease.

"Yup! And like someone reminded me earlier, shame is usually someone else's problem. I'm not ashamed of hating horror films at all!"

When we get into the apartment Malachi sits on one end of the couch and I sit on the other with a cushion on top of my lap and plenty of space between us. We watch a Kevin Hart comedy and chat through the commercials about school and music. I tell him about the empty houses that have begun appearing on the block and how quickly they are being bought up. When the movie ends at ten Malachi gets up and puts his jacket on without my asking him to.

"Thanks for answering my call today, Santi." He leans down and wraps his long arms around me, and I feel warmth shoot from the middle of my back where he hugs me all the way up to my face. I hug him tightly back.

Trouble. This boy is just straight trouble.

RAMIFICATIONS

My cell phone rings the next morning just as 'Buela is headed out to church. " 'Buela, can you get that? My hands are wet," I call when I hear her coming down the steps. I'm at the sink washing the pans I let soak overnight. Sometimes, Babygirl and I go with her to church, but she never presses me if I'm not ready or don't want to go. Today is one of those days where I'm looking forward to enjoying a playful and easy morning with my kid.

The phone stops ringing and I hear 'Buela murmur into it, "Sí, one moment, Tyrone."

'Buela hands me a towel and holds my phone out to me. I dry my hands and take it from her, conscious that she hasn't left but has decided to rest against the doorframe. That can't be good.

I take a deep breath. "Hey, Tyrone. Wassup?"

"Yo, Emoni, why am I getting phone calls from one of my boys telling me he saw you walk into your house with some dude? I miss one weekend with her, and you bringing other guys around my daughter?"

I close my eyes. *This* cannot be what he's calling me about. Why does he have people in my neighborhood checking for me, anyway? Furthermore, what business is it of his? Especially if Babygirl didn't even meet Malachi?

I ball up the dish towel but after a glance at 'Buela smooth it out. I don't want her to see I'm upset.

"I didn't bring anyone around your daughter," I say, and shoot another look at 'Buela. She raises an eyebrow and walks into the living room. "And if I have a friend from school come over to help me with a side project, that's my business."

Tyrone's voice is harsh in reply. "Working on a 'side project' is a funny way to say you're someone's side piece."

My breath gets short in my chest. I can't believe Tyrone sometimes. "Tyrone, he wasn't around your daughter. She was asleep. She never met him. And I don't have to explain myself to you."

"Your grandmother was there?" Tyrone asks.

I force myself to inhale deeply, then exhale the same way before I respond. I try to remember that what's best for Babygirl isn't always what's easiest for me. Because right now what would be easy is to hang up on Tyrone. "Yes, 'Buela was home."

"Put her on. I want to ask her myself."

I walk into the living room and stop halfway to the couch. Nah. I don't ask about the girls he dates and I don't harrass him when he says he doesn't introduce them to Babygirl. Plus, we aren't children anymore; our parents aren't going to sign us out of trouble.

"Tyrone, I'm not putting my grand-mother on. I have never lied to you."

He breathes hard in my ear, then all sound drops from the call. He's hung up on me. Babygirl is sitting in 'Buela's lap, sucking her thumb.

"Why don't you get her dressed?" 'Buela asks. "At this rate I'll have missed the procession by the time I get to the church — and I don't like walking in late. We can go get breakfast instead. We'll do those dishes later."

I know the smile I've forced onto my face wobbles at the edges, but I keep it pinned on and I keep my tears to myself.

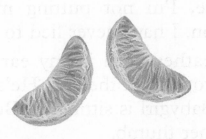

CAFÉ SORREL

When 'Buela, Babygirl, and I have an excursion, the getting-ready part is always a production. Toss in that my hands are still shaking from my conversation with Tyrone, and I'm moving in slow motion just to iron one blouse. By the time we have Babygirl strapped into the stroller and exit the house, it's already noon.

We don't go out to eat much. When I was younger, we used to visit the local restaurants for holidays and birthdays or after going to the cemetery to visit with my grandfather or moms. But that was a long while ago, before 'Buela stopped working. Now the only time we have outside food is if I bring something in from the Burger Joint or when Tyrone and I used to go on dates. Otherwise it's on me or 'Buela to cook.

Today I'm surprised when 'Buela heads to the train. We go to a spot in Rittenhouse Square called Café Sorrel. The napkins are made of cloth and the flowers in the vases are real and fresh. The hostess asks if we need a booster seat, and I realize that Babygirl has never been in a high-class restaurant. When the server arrives, I notice everything he does, including the way he straightens the knife and salad fork, and how he folds our napkins into a triangle and gently holds them out for us to place on our laps, and how elegantly he pours water into our glasses.

"This is really fancy, 'Buela," I say when the server walks away. I trace the delicate embroidery on the edge of the tablecloth.

"Yes, I like this place." 'Buela takes a sip of her water. And well, that doesn't make any sense. This place looks new, and when would 'Buela have ever had the occasion to come eat here? I open my mouth to ask but the server has circled back with our menus.

"We have a fall special with the following dishes . . ."

He reads off his notepad and I close my eyes when he describes how each dish is prepared. I want to memorize everything.

"You order, nena. This is all you." 'Buela turns to the server. "My granddaughter is taking a culinary arts class. She is amazing in the kitchen."

"Oh" — the server raises an eyebrow — "how lovely. You're going to have to let us know what you think of the meal." I have a feeling he's probably a college student at Penn or Temple and couldn't care less what I think; he's simply being overly friendly to get that tip. So, no, I don't plan on giving him my opinion on anything.

I take a look at the menu and keep my smile on my face even though the prices drop-kick me in the gut. I look for the cheapest items on the menu, then smile up at the server.

"May I have the duck appetizer on the bed of risotto? My grandmother will have the partridge. And can we have pommes frites for this little one?" I gesture to Babygirl, who gives a huge smile and bangs on the table.

The server removes our menus and stacks them in his arms. "Very well, your bread is on its way."

Buela neatly folds and refolds the napkin in her lap. "Those sounded like very nice orders. How is class going? I haven't heard you mention any special quizzes lately," 'Buela asks, and sips her water.

She knows. I can see it in her face that she knows. "Who told you?"

"Told me what, nena?" 'Buela says. She smiles at the busboy, who sets a basket of bread on the table. He has a tattoo of the Puerto Rican flag on his neck, and although 'Buela hates tattoos, she loves her island. I bet she'll pass him a tip later. "Oh, lord, m'ijo. Bringing us all this bread! I haven't been walking as much as I used to. This bread is going to go straight to my hips," she says as she grabs a roll and breaks it in half. She gives the other half to Babygirl, who bites into it with enthusiasm. The busboy smiles at her.

"And what would be the point of hips if we couldn't enjoy bread every now and then?" the busboy says in Spanish. And although this whole exchange is cute, I need him to walk away. As soon as he does, I pounce again.

"I know you know I've been skipping class. It's written all over your face. Who said something?"

'Buela takes a huge bite of bread and makes me wait until she's done chewing to speak. "What is most important is that *you* didn't tell me."

Angelica must have found out somehow. Or maybe Ms. Fuentes saw last week's attendance sheet and called home.

"You've never had an issue with attendance, not even when you were pregnant. It seems to me like you were really excited about the class for a while and maybe when it got hard you got scared about the challenge."

I look away from 'Buela, and use my napkin to wipe crumbs from Babygirl's chin. 'Buela reaches across and stills my hand. "I'm not saying I don't understand. Or that I don't know you well enough to say that you've climbed higher hills. I only mean to say, I hope you didn't sell yourself short."

I squeeze her hand. "I haven't dropped the class entirely yet."

"So are you going to go back?"

I shrug and look down at my plate where I've crumbled a bread roll into nothing but dust. 'Buela takes the hint. "Tell me about your other classes."

She listens as I tell her about physics and English. About the college essay I'm working on. When the food comes out the scents fill my nostrils and I close my eyes and inhale deeply.

"What's this with my bird?" 'Buela points.

"Polenta," I say, and take a bite of my risotto. I close my eyes again and savor. Basil, cream . . . and a pop of something. I take another bite but still can't place it. 'Buela says something and I chew slowly, trying to hear her past the rush in my ears.

"What'd you say?" I ask, when I come back to earth.

"I was saying, this is really good. How is yours?"

"Too good. I can't wait to try it at home." Babygirl murmurs agreement

231

through a mouth full of fries.

"So how was it, miss?" the server asks as he takes away the plates.

"Really good." And although I said I wasn't going to say anything, I can't keep the question to myself. "There was something in the risotto. Not the basil or cream or mushroom but something else?"

The server shakes his head with a puzzled look, crinkling his forehead. "I'm not sure. No other ingredients are listed on the menu."

I hope my annoyance doesn't show on my face. "Oh. Okay."

'Buela smiles. "May I have a coffee and the check?"

"Very well," the server says.

"Yumyumyum." Babygirl hums under her breath and I offer her water. She takes a sip and lets it dribble down her chin and grins.

"Emma!" I look up when I feel someone behind my shoulder, hoping it's the server so I can ask for another napkin, but my eyes land on a buttoned-up white jacket, a woman's smiling face beneath a chef's hat. "Everything good here, ladies?"

'Buela and I nod. "Very good. I enjoyed the polenta!" 'Buela says, and holds up her forefinger touching her thumb. I try not to groan at how excited she sounds.

"I heard there was a question about the risotto?" The chef looks at me.

My mouth goes dry. Even though I don't know this lady, I'm starstruck by the jacket, by the Crocs and checkered pants. By the food that melted in my mouth and looked almost too pretty to eat. Chefs rarely leave their kitchens so I know it's a big deal she decided to answer me in person.

"Umm." Get it together, Emoni! "I tasted the basil, and cream. What might have been cremini mushrooms? But there was something else. At the back of my tongue . . . I couldn't place it," I say, and blush. I sound as silly as 'Buela.

"Ah, probably the orange zest. It's just a hint. Most people can't even taste it but it adds a bright note." She cocks her head to the side.

"Oh! Orange zest." I close my eyes and

run my tongue along my teeth. Try to remember the flavor. "Yeah, that feels right. Orange zest."

My eyes pop open. The server comes back and hands the check to 'Buela, who immediately swoops it under the table so I can't see it.

"Chef, did the young lady tell you? She's taking a culinary arts class," the server says, and takes the check back from 'Buela with her payment.

"Are you? At the Institute?"

I shake my head. "At my high school. It just started this year with a new instructor."

Her eyes sharpen on my face and I almost lean back from the intensity of her look. "Wait a minute, a friend of mine just started teaching a cooking class at a high school. You don't go to a charter school near here, by any chance?"

Before I can answer 'Buela chimes in. "She does! Emoni goes to Schomburg Charter School about fifteen minutes from here on the bus. Is your friend Chef Ayden?"

The chef claps her hands together and

laughs. "What a small world — one of Ayden's students coming into my restaurant. You have a good instructor; Ayden is one of a kind. . . . Kind of a hard-ass, but he'll teach you a lot." Her eyes twinkle when she says it and I can tell she and Chef Ayden must know each other well.

And just in case they are friends, I keep my mouth shut about his hard-ass-ness.

She smiles at me again. "You have the taste buds, and married with the technique and work ethic you're learning in class, you'll acquire the holy trinity to make it in this industry. I need to get back to my kitchen, but don't worry about today's bill." She waves at the server to bring the bill back. "It's on me. Let Ayden know it was a pleasure to meet one of his students."

I hear her chuckling under her breath as she walks away.

From: E.Santiago@schs.edu
To: SarahFowlkes_15@exchange.com
Date: Sunday, October 6, 10:31 PM
Subject: re: recipe

Hey Aunt Sarah,
I'm glad to hear that by the time the storm touched down near you it was mostly rain and nothing too bad. I kept my eye on the news all week and kept hoping the family would be okay. My father says the worst of the storm missed them, but I know there were power outages on the western side of the island. It was nice of you to ask how you could help; my father says they are accepting donations of boxes of canned food and bottled water. I'm attaching the information link at the end of the email.

Thanks for your last recipe for fried green tomatoes. The story of how you and my momma used to eat the green tomatoes straight from the vine made me smile. I can't believe it was so easy for you to just walk into your back-yard and pick them, especially since I

struggled to find them in my neighborhood! The vendors at the vegetable
stands kept looking at me like I was
stupid, but I finally found some at a
farmer's market on the other side of
the city.

But, let me tell you, the journey was
worth it! Them things were delicious!
I fried them like you said, but I used
a little bit of panko breadcrumbs in
the dredge. Then I paired them with
queso frito and some basil, and it was
like a homestyle take on caprese salad.

I'm going to try the recipe again this
week and I'll send you my remix once
I have it exactly right. Thanks again
for the invite to come down during
Christmas break. I don't think I can
travel down on the bus with Babygirl
by myself, and I wouldn't want to
leave her, but I hope to make it down
sometime.

        With love & cinnamon dust,

                  E

TASTE BUDS

Although my Sunday was transformed from a clustermess into a nice memory, Monday rolls around and I've overslept, Babygirl is late for daycare, and 'Buela keeps chewing my head off about the smallest things, and by the time I make it to the bus stop I've missed Angelica and Advisory. And what doesn't help my bad mood is that I still haven't made a decision about Culinary Arts. I have one period after lunch to decide whether I'm going to go or not, and I know that if I tack on too many more absences I'm going to have to drop the class simply because I'll be failing it. I don't know what I'm going to do, but luckily lunch rolls around and I have Angelica to take my mind off any decisions.

By the time I meet up with her at our table she's visibly trembling with excitement.

"You don't understand, Emoni. It was *so* perfect."

I nod and smile. "Tell me everything. Why was it so perfect?"

"So it was perfect not just because of the movie Laura streamed, which was funny and romantic. Or the deep conversations we had, or the wine Laura brought from her father's house. I was so nervous I was giggling and Laura just reached out and . . . well, that part was perfect, too. All of it."

Something inside me stops laughing at her dreamy expression. My girl is truly in love and I'm choked up at having been a part of making that night special for her.

"Emoni, the food? I've had your cooking a dozen times, but there was one point where Laura and I both put our forks down and just grinned like little kids because we were so happy. And I think the meal had something to do with it because I had some of the leftovers last night and I just felt all warm and fuzzy and loved inside. If I ever have that chimi-chimi sauce again, I'll think of that night."

I laugh. "It's chimi*churri* sauce, Angelica. And I'm glad you liked it. I told you I put a little extra heat in it, and it sounds like you added more than enough spice to the rest of the night."

And then I'm struck stupid because in all the time I've known her, I've never seen Angelica blush. But she does. Her brown skin warms up with a tinge of pink in the cheeks as she snorts on her sandwich.

NEW BEGINNINGS

When the bell rings for my last class before Culinary Arts, I'm out the door with the quickness. I want to get there before any of the other students. By the time I arrive at class I'm out of breath and huffing, but I still make sure not to slam the door behind me.

Chef Ayden looks up with a start when he hears my heavy breathing. I can't read the look on his face. Inscrutable, Ms. Fuentes would call it.

"Emoni, long time." Chef Ayden closes his laptop with a soft click. He stuffs his hands into his soft, checkered chef's pants. "We missed you last week."

"I just . . . I'm not a quitter. I didn't understand why you were asking me to throw away food or follow the recipe exactly even though my instincts told me it would taste better differently. I didn't get it. But I think I do now. And I wanted to say . . ."

What did I want to say?

Chef waits. The moment stretches into the yard beyond awkward and enters the goal post of embarrassing. He raises his right eyebrow.

I clear my throat and I know my face is burning. "I wanted to say, I promise to work hard. To try my best to follow directions. Because I think about creating food all the time and even though I know a lot . . . I can learn more. I went to a restaurant over the weekend; the head chef says she knows you? It was Café Sorrel. Seeing her in her coat, and tasting her food, it not only made me realize I want to keep getting my technique down in this class, it made me realize I can be like her one day — an executive chef."

Chef doesn't say anything. He just keeps blinking at me with his head cocked. My chest deflates. I don't think he can kick me out of class, not with only four absences. But I also don't want him to hate me. I swallow back a knot that collects in my throat. Look down at the long metal table where we present our dishes. I missed being in class, and I didn't know how much until this moment.

"Lisa is an excellent chef. I'm glad you were able to try her food. As for your absences, we've been looking for someone in class to lead the fund-raising campaign for the trip to Spain. One day you might own a restaurant, or be head chef, and honing your leadership skills now will be useful. Would you like to head that committee?"

I hear everything he's saying, but it's like each piece of information is a bit of colored glass and I need hold it up to the light to see how it shines. Chef Ayden isn't angry with me. Chef Ayden thinks I could own or be head chef of a restaurant one day. Chef Ayden wants me to lead a fund-raising committee.

I've seen chefs on TV time and time again say they had to pay their dues. And I never knew exactly what that meant but now I think I get it. It's about doing the grunt work behind the scenes, washing dishes, folding napkins, taking stock, before you ever touch a recipe. It's about being the creative mind behind raising a shit-ton of money so you can go on a trip abroad.

I hold my hand out. Chef looks at it and shakes it, super serious.

He pats me on the shoulder. "You've got what it takes, Emoni. I don't doubt that if you keep yourself focused and your knives sharp, you'll be running a kitchen one day. I won't treat you any different from anyone else just because you have something special, but let's both take a moment to acknowledge that you've got what it takes."

I put on my jacket, my scarf, and my game face. I've got what it takes.

Guess Who's Back?

When the rest of the class walks into the room, most of the students don't seem surprised to see me — they must have just thought I was absent. Malachi raises an eyebrow and his lips perk up on one end. We haven't talked since Saturday. We texted a little on Sunday, but after the phone call with Tyrone, talking with Malachi lost some of its glow. I look away from him to where Pretty Leslie cuts her eyes at me then inspects her nails. Passion-fruit purple, I'd name them. I go to my old station but Chef flags me down.

"Over here, Emoni. You will work with

Richard and Amanda. As a trio. I think you'll work better as part of a team." He claps his hands together. "Okay, everyone, your recipes are on your boards."

I walk over to Richard and Amanda and offer a weak smile. Richard smiles back and Amanda tightens her cap. I run a hand down my jacket front; it feels good to be back in uniform. The next hour passes by in a blur. I spend the majority of the time listening to Amanda and Richard as they ask me to dice, chop, and sauté root vegetables. I pay more attention to the little details than the overall dish. By the time everything is plated I'm surprised at what it actually is. The chicken breast is perfectly cooked, and the thinly sliced carrots look beautiful underneath it, and although I didn't have anything to do with the seasoning or the plating, I'm proud of how the whole dish came together. Even if I would have used a bit of balsamic vinegar in the sauce.

We place the plate in front of Chef and he scoops a clean fork from his bowl and tries it. "Very good. Very, very good. Well done, *team.*"

I roll my eyes at him and he winks at

me as he shoos us away so the next group can be graded. As class lets out I glance at Malachi's station, but he's already gone. I'm halfway down the hall when an arm comes around my shoulder and with a loud smack a kiss is placed on my left temple.

"Glad to have you back, Santi," Malachi says with a grin that I return.

"Glad to be back."

VISITATIONS

The rest of the school week goes by quickly and before I know it, it's Saturday morning.

"Babygirl, hold still," I say, tugging her little Jordans onto her feet. She keeps wriggling around, trying to climb up to Tyrone. "Can you help, please?"

I've been trying to get her dressed for more than five minutes, and he's just been sitting across from me like a dodo bird. Fine, he's still mad about the Malachi thing, but lord knows he has all kinds of girls up in his house, so why he's hung up on my friends is beyond me. He didn't even say hello to 'Buela, and she has nothing to do with this. As much as his mother loves sticking her nose in the air, some days Tyrone has no damn home training.

Finally he lets go a long sigh. "Emma, let your mom put your stuff on." But Emma tugs her foot, flipping the sneaker up, and it bangs me in the nose.

"Ouch! Emma!" Babygirl looks up, startled at her government name springing from my lips, and starts to cry.

"Here, let me help," 'Buela says, and picks up Babygirl and the sneaker. "I'm going to take her onto my bed; it might be easier to get her dressed there." She raises an eyebrow and gives me a pointed look. I know what she's thinking: She doesn't like it when Tyrone and I are mad at each other. She says it's bad for Babygirl because she gets stuck in the middle.

I stop rubbing my nose and take a deep breath. "You still feel some type of way? Let's just go ahead and talk about it."

Tyrone readjusts the brim of his fitted. "I don't have anything to say."

Which is clearly a lie. Tyrone knows so many words to sweet-talk a girl, but when it comes to talking about his feelings he always swears he has nothing to say. "You turned eighteen a couple of months ago, which means you're an adult. We can talk like grown-ups. So, why are you angry?

You date girls all the time. And this wasn't even a date. He's just a friend."

He shakes his head. "Maaan, 'a friend,' who I don't know, who was around my daughter."

"Is that why you're actually angry? You tell me about every girl who meets you at the playground when you have Babygirl with you? Or the shopping-mall trips you go on that aren't dates, but somehow, photos get posted on social media of you and girls and my daughter asleep in a stroller? Thing one, he's new to Philadelphia, so you'd have no reason to know him. Thing two, Tyrone, we have a child. We can't play silent-treatment games. For the rest of our lives, God willing, we'll have a child. So, I can't afford to act like one and neither can you."

And it must be true when they say you become your parents, because that lecture could have been stolen straight from 'Buela's script.

Tyrone tugs his fitted down so it covers his eyes and I know it's not because the light slanting in through the window bothers him. He looks like a puppy that got in trouble for peeing on the rug. "We decided we weren't going to stay together for the baby. Fine, I get that. But you said you weren't going to date other people."

If he were Angelica, I would hold his hand and use my soft voice that I take on when I hurt her feelings. If he were 'Buela, I would take a deep breath and use my "I'm an adult" voice that is slow and patient. But he's neither of those people, and I still haven't figured out what voice to use when he's hurt but also being illogical. So instead, I choose my words with slow care. "I'm not dating other people. But that doesn't mean I can't, does it? I think if you have people in my neighborhood making sure your daughter is safe, that's good. That makes you a good father. But if you have people spying on me to see whether or not I bring dudes home, that's going to hurt you more than it's going to hurt me. And it's going to hurt Emma most." I feel my voice hitch in my throat. Tyrone and I have had many talks but never one like this.

Tyrone doesn't speak again. He stands when 'Buela comes into the room.

251

"Thanks, Mrs. Santiago. I appreciate you getting Emma ready," he says, taking Babygirl from 'Buela's arms.

He grabs the baby bag and the stroller while still holding Babygirl on his hip. I open the door for him and kiss Babygirl on the cheek, and can't help but get a whiff of Tyrone. He smells like soap and fresh aftershave.

"Don't let your mom feed her too many granola bars, please? I know they seem healthy, but they are full of sugar."

"I won't." He leans in and has Babygirl plant a kiss on my cheek. It's the closest he'll get to offering an apology. Babygirl seems happy in his arms and doesn't stir when she realizes 'Buela and I are staying behind.

"I'll have her back right on time tomorrow," Tyrone calls over his shoulder.

I close the door and lean against it. 'Buela begins picking up the playthings that Babygirl had spread across the floor.

"It's a hard path you're walking, Emoni. But you're doing just fine. Now, come help me clean your daughter's clutter."

I shake my head at all the separate feelings inside me; sometimes I feel more scattered than Babygirl's toys.

PROPOSALS

Over the next week and a half, as part of my new role as head of the fund-raising committee, I have to submit a list of ideas to Chef Ayden that will help us raise the eight thousand dollars needed for our trip. I talk it over with Angelica, and her creative mind spins with big galas and silent auctions of her artwork. She even suggests reaching out to local rappers and asking them to give proceeds of their record sales for the trip. When I ask Malachi for his thoughts, he goes in a different direction than Angelica; like the doctor he's told me he wants to be, he talks about the optimal results and makes a bullet-point list of how to make the most money in the quickest fashion. 'Buela taps on her chin when I ask her and thinks of a bingo game at the rec center with all proceeds going to the trip. I've been calling Julio more often since the storm, and he's quick to offer his thoughts on organizing a fund-raiser. He gives me a letter template to petition our district council member and has a whole game plan outlined for me to knock on doors in the neighborhood with food samples so people will donate directly. He says the best way to move forward is to keep it grassroots; when you support the community, the community will support you.

I make detailed notes of everyone's suggestions and on my own I spend time in the computer lab after school looking up different ways to raise money. I feel a thrill in my body; I'm excited to put my proposal in motion. I know we can make this work. But first I'll have to convince Chef Ayden.

Angelica helps me write up my presentation with graphics and pie charts, and Malachi checks my numbers to make sure all the math is correct. 'Buela and

Babygirl listen as I practice presenting my proposal. Although I'm the chairperson, this is my unofficial committee, and like Chef Ayden always says, sometimes you need a team to help you.

I'm standing in front of Chef Ayden. I've printed out neat copies of my ideas, the timeline, and the projected amount we'll raise.

"As you see from my list, there are a couple of options. I know the class has thought of a bake sale and I think we should do that to raise money, but not for the class trip. I think we should use it to raise money to buy larger quantities of food to cook in class for us to sell. This very kitchen has the small café next door. Instead of using it for restaurant practice, I think we should open it up and serve lunch. We have all this food that we make but that goes to waste. Why not make larger portions and sell them for more money than we spent on the food? It would only require buying larger amounts, storing the food appropriately throughout the week, and making sure the recipes are ones we can sell. I'm sure the staff would like to have options for something other than the cafeteria food."

Chef raises an eyebrow. What I'm asking will mean more work for him, mainly picking up and storing bigger quantities of food weekly. "I also think we should submit a proposal to the school to have us cater the Winter Dinner."

I stop speaking and look down at my notes. Chef Ayden pauses before asking me, "The cafeteria staff usually does the Winter Dinner, don't they?"

"We all need to learn how to serve, and that would be a great opportunity. We can propose it as one of the objectives: on-the-job experience."

Chef cocks his head. "You've thought about this a lot, Emoni. I'm impressed. Except, the only class advanced enough to make acceptable food to feed to staff would be yours, and you all meet in the afternoon. If we want the lunch idea to work, people will have to come in early to cook. Do you think you can lead that?"

I hadn't counted on more work. But I puff up my chest. I got this.

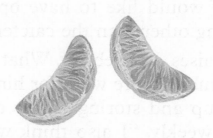

THE BRIGHT SIDE

" 'Buela?" I call from the kitchen doorway as I dry off the freshly washed dishes.

I hear her chanclas shuffling down from her room. "M'ija? What's going on? Baby Emma is asleep."

I try not to let the disappointment show on my face. "Oh, I didn't know you'd put her down. I didn't get to say good night." I glance at the microwave clock. When did it get past ten?

'Buela rests against the doorframe. "She dozed off. You know she has all that energy, running around, and then she eats, and boom, fast asleep. Pass me a rag so I can help with those."

"Only a few left — I got them. I actually wanted to talk to you about something else. The trip to Spain. Even though

I'm not sure if I'll be able to raise enough to cover my portion, if I can pay for it I'm still not sure what I'll do with Babygirl that week. I didn't want to assume you would take on her care all by yourself."

'Buela takes the rag from me and folds it up in a neat little square. "You want to ask for help from Tyrone and his family?"

I shake my head. "Tyrone has school and his parents work complicated hospital hours. They wouldn't be able to pick her up and drop her off at daycare."

'Buela sighs. "This *is* a big deal. I always wanted to travel, you know? I've only ever seen my island and Philadelphia. I said after retirement that your grandfather and me would see the world. And then he died, and, well." She opens her hands as if in prayer. "And here we are. You may never get this opportunity again. I can call Tyrone's parents, and between us, we can work out a schedule. Let's think of it as a graduation present? Emoni, nena, speaking of graduation — you know I'm so proud of you, right? But you're going to have to figure out what happens next. Have you gotten those school applications in? And that FAFSA form thing?"

I reach out and give 'Buela a tight hug, inhaling her familiar scent. She's right, about all of it. I have a lot of decisions to make, but tonight I'm going to dream about cooking, and Spain, and graduation.

TEAM PLAYER

"Emoni, can you blanch the asparagus and season it?" Richard calls from where he's chopping onions. Amanda is absent today and I've been standing back less and helping out more. It's hard to keep my hands from just *doing,* but Richard makes sure we stay on track, following the recipe down to the last half teaspoon.

I set the pot of water to boil and slice through the asparagus the way the recipe says.

Over his shoulder, Richard calls out the next instruction. "Oh, and the orzo, that needs to get going."

Again, I nod, and get the necessary ingredients from the pantry. Richard is a heavyset kid who wears an oversized

261

jacket and has the cutest little mole over his lip. I think his family is Polish, but Richard is straight Philly, from his haircut to his sneakers. We work down to the wire with him calling instructions and me trying to ensure I don't do anything I'm not supposed to. Today is a testing day, which means that anything we place in front of Chef will be graded, *plus* we need to be able to answer questions about each of our dishes. Richard and Amanda always do well and I don't want to mess up their track record. I measure the necessary salt and grind the fresh peppercorn, and squeeze only so much lemon. The garnish is the exact amount of thyme called for.

Across the room, Malachi has finished plating and is cleaning up his station, rapping underneath his breath. Leslie swings her hips and mimes being in front of a microphone. I look away from them, and Richard and I approach Chef. He turns the dish in several circles before sticking his fork in, closing his eyes.

"Asparagus is good, orzo is right. Skirt steak is right." He opens his eyes. "The dish needs a little more salt, but otherwise, well done. I knew you could pull it off." And although he is talking to Richard and me, I have a feeling the comment was for me.

Chef looks at me. "What's the correct ratio of water to orzo?"

I answer him. He asks Richard a question about the temperature to cook a steak medium rare.

Another group stands behind us waiting to approach Chef, and I try to bite back the words bubbling in my mouth, but like a covered pot of boiling water, they spill over. "You need to change your measurement."

Chef looks up from his grading. "Excuse me?"

I point to the recipe. "Your measurement of salt in the recipe, we followed it exactly. So if the dish needs more salt, you need to change your measurement."

He raises an eyebrow and as we walk to our station, Richard elbows me in the ribs. "Seriously, Emoni? You couldn't just let it go?"

I don't answer. Call me salty.

COVEN

"Angelica, where did you get all of this stuff?" I ask her as she bursts through the door carrying bags and bags of fabric. She's changed her hair to a black bob but the ends are bright pink.

Angelica really is like one of those tropical storms we keep getting warnings about on the news, swirling until she descends in a pile of mayhem. "You know that Laura works for the theater at her school. She gets access to all the extra fabric from the set. She hooked us up! And not a moment too soon, since Halloween is only a week away."

Angelica sets the bags down and walks to where Babygirl sits on the couch in front of the TV, where she's been spooning mashed potatoes into her mouth. I finger a piece of gold spandex peeking out from one of the bags.

"Oh my God. Babygirl isn't even three yet. She's not big enough for a costume to need this much material. What are we going to do with all of it?"

"Make her the best damn — I mean, darn — costume anyone has ever seen."

"Angelica, I told you I don't even think I can take her trick-or-treating." I shuffle from one foot to the other. "And she needs to go to bed soon."

"Me and your grandmother will figure out trick-or-treating. She's not my godbaby for nothing, right, Em?" Angelica leans down and blows kisses onto Babygirl's feet.

"Hola, Angelica," 'Buela says. She's wearing pink pj's and her hair is up in rollers. It'd be late for any other friend to come over, but this is Angelica.

"¡Bendición, Abuela Gloria!" Angelica sings out. She hugs 'Buela so tight that they're swaying.

"Que Dios te bendiga, m'ija." 'Buela dances with Angelica for a moment before gesturing to the bags with her chin. "What's all this?"

"We're going to make a costume for Babygirl. Aren't we, Babygirl?"

"Ah, bueno. It's getting late and she needs to be going to bed, no? Why don't I help? I can take measurements quicker than you two put together."

Angelica pulls out the measuring tape and her design notebook. She starts flipping through the book with her fuschia-tipped hair swinging.

"I was thinking we could do a doctor! Or maybe even an astronaut! A Chiquita Banana girl with a fruit crown? It all depends on what you want. What should it be?"

'Buela chimes in, "A beauty queen? Or how about a movie star? Como la Audrey Hepburn."

I look at Babygirl, patiently spooning food into her mouth like she hasn't a care in the world. And suddenly I know exactly what she should be for Halloween. "I think it'd be cute if she was a chef. With a little smock, and a hat, checkered pants, and a spatula. Maybe even some of those little clogs. She could be 'cooking' up a bowl of popcorn."

Angelica snaps her fingers. "Yes! That's so cute! Maybe you can put on your chef jacket and take a picture before you go to work."

"A chef," 'Buela says, a smile lighting up her face. "That's perfect. And maybe Cheerios instead of popcorn!"

All of a sudden the three of us are pulling fabric out, and 'Buela has grabbed the measuring tape. Angelica clicks on a playlist on her phone. We all smile at Babygirl, who shows off her teeth as if she knows she has a coven of women holding her down, and that she can be anything and everything we dream for her.

DREAMS

I sometimes wonder what my mother might have dreamed for me if she hadn't died when I was born. If she would have wanted me to be a doctor or a lawyer, if she would have been pushier to ensure I did better in school. I love 'Buela, and I'm so lucky to have her, but as supportive as she is, 'Buela isn't the type to run down to a school and smack a counselor upside the head for discouraging me from applying somewhere. 'Buela isn't the type to demand the school test me to see why I get so mixed up with directions or struggled to speak early on. 'Buela walks through the world with her hands palms up; she takes what's given to her in stride and never complains or cries.

I dream every single day for Babygirl. I see people in business suits on the bus, and I imagine Babygirl grown up with a briefcase and a nice executive office job. I watch a TV show and imagine Babygirl as a famous actress winning an Oscar. There's so much I want for her that sometimes I think the seams of my skin aren't enough to contain every hope I have. And I whisper it to her all the time. When I'm feeding her. When she's asleep in my arms. When we are playing at the park. I whisper all the everything I know she can be and the ways I'll fight for her to be them. I want her to know her entire life her mommy may not have had a powerful job or made millions, but that her moms did everything so that she could be an accumulation of the best dreams.

From: E.Santiago@schs.edu
To: SarahFowlkes_15@exchange.com
Date: Friday, November 1, 8:18 PM
Subject: Pics

Hey Aunt Sarah,
I hope you're good! I've kept playing around with that recipe you sent me for your mac and cheese. I've attached a picture of it plated. I added some gruyère cheese and it was finger-licking good.

I also attached a picture of Babygirl for Halloween. Isn't her apron the cutest? I wasn't able to go trick-or-treating with her, but 'Buela and Angelica took her all around the neighborhood and to the rec center, where there was a contest for best costume in different age groups. Unfortunately, she lost to an infant T'Challa, but next year we are going to plan in advance and we will win that contest, Wakanda or no Wakanda.

I appreciate you sending some ideas for the fund-raiser. I actually need one more thing from you . . . do you think you can send me the family's version for stuffing? I have an idea I think I could use to raise money.

With all my love & some cinnamon
dust,
E

Every Day I'm Hustling

It's been two weeks since I turned the proposal in, but finally Chef Ayden and the school administration have approved my fund-raising plan, and I officially have a new schedule that's taken over my life. I wake up an hour and a half earlier than I used to, before the sun has even blinked awake, and get ready for school. The guards know two of us have special permission three mornings out of the week to be let into the kitchen early, where Chef waits to start the lunch special for the day. Although he never said anything, I know he had to argue with the principal on our behalf to reopen the small training restaurant attached to the downstairs kitchen.

Us students rotate so no one has to show up more than once a week, but if someone can't make it, I fill in since I'm the fund-raising lead. In the afternoons, a different student volunteers to be the lunchtime server for the three different lunch periods; each day after school for a whole week one student washes the dishes and helps Chef Ayden clean the restaurant. Since people are getting extra cooking time in the morning, it should work out that everyone ultimately learns the same number of recipes.

I expected teachers would want the option of another food spot in the building, but I never expected the little restaurant to be full every single shift. Most days we run out of everything we've made and Chef has to turn people away. And at a profit of seven dollars a pop for a meal, and about ten to twelve teachers per lunch period, three lunch periods a day, we're raising just shy of seven hundred dollars a week and have five weeks still left to go until our December deadline. I've done the math over and over, but it still comes out that we'll hit about three thousand five hundred dollars by the Winter Dinner. I try not let my nervousness over how much we need to raise show when I give weekly updates to the class, but I know I have to do everything in my power to get as many people at the dinner as the gym will hold.

And putting all this effort at school isn't easy. I'm still working hours at the Burger Joint, going to tutoring after school for math, and spending as much time with Babygirl as I can manage.

Before I know it, the first two months of school have flown by and we are in the middle of November. Which means that the Winter Dinner is coming up. And how much money we raise by December doesn't just determine whether the class can go to Spain, it determines whether my ideas and sweat and time have mattered. Which means I can't fail.

OUT OF THE FRYING PAN

I'm in the kitchen one early morning sticking some bread rolls in the oven. After I set the timer, I clean my station and look around the room. Pretty Leslie is stirring a massive pot of chicken-noodle soup, and Richard is slicing up tomatoes, onions, and lettuce for sand-wich fixings.

Chef sits at a small desk in the corner, and I know this is my chance.

"Chef, I was wondering if I could speak to you?" He takes a second to look up from his computer and I see he has bags under his eyes. I've never wondered if Chef is married, or has kids, or how far he lives from school. And unlike us, he's been getting up every single morning to be here early and lead the kitchen, and he often stays after school to prep for the next day.

"What's up, Emoni? Everything good with your bread?"

I nod. "I had some ideas for this year's Winter Dinner. Some ways we could flip it so it's something new that people who come every year haven't seen."

He closes his laptop and gives me his full attention. "How so?"

"Well, they always do some canned ham and some simple ole green beans. The exact kinds of things people make at home for the holiday. But what if we made it more restaurant style? Like a chorizo bite on a bed of herbed stuffing? Or individual portions of baked mac and cheese?"

Chef temples his fingers together. "What would you do to elevate the mac and cheese?"

I place a hand on my chest, offended. "Absolutely nothing. Baked mac and cheese doesn't need elevation, degradation, hateration, or nothing else. It's perfect in its purest form. Although we could add some gouda."

Chef grins. "I love it. Why don't you write up some ideas and we'll figure out the measurements and portions."

I walk back to the bread rolls, which have risen in the oven and filled the kitchen with the warmest smell. I'm creating a menu for hundreds of people. I feel like something has risen inside me, too, and it tastes a bit like hope.

CRUNCH TIME

Thanksgiving is a week away, and two weeks after that is the Winter Dinner. We have only a handful of weeks to finish raising the money for Spain. The lunch sales have been going steady and we are almost at twenty-five hundred dollars. But winter break is coming, and the deposit is due a few days after the Winter Dinner.

Even though he tries to look super chill, I know Chef is nervous that we still have over six thousand dollars to raise. The school will pay us a thousand for the Winter Dinner, but that still leaves too much we might not be able to raise in December alone. I've sure gotten a lot better at math since I've taken on tallying up our sales every week to see where we are in the fund-raising.

When I walk into class the third week in November, I see that there are no recipes on our boards. I button up my jacket and stand next to Richard. "Today we're going to come up with some creative solutions to the problem we are having. Emoni has been doing a great job brainstorming ideas to raise money, but I think this last push needs a collective effort. We want to go to Sevilla, yes?"

As if our heads are attached to puppet strings, we all nod.

Malachi raises his hand. "What if we built onto what we already have? I don't know how the Winter Dinner is done every year, but wouldn't that be a good time to do more than just cater?"

"My father does landscaping," Richard says. "What if we auctioned off his services? People donate money for that sort of thing, right?"

Amanda nods. "What if we also made the dinner open to the public, not just family and friends? My sister has over thirty thousand followers on Instagram and I'm sure my parents would promote it to their clients. If we moved it to the gym instead of the cafeteria we could fit more tables."

No one I know can offer much but I begin taking neat notes of the suggestions. Chef Ayden claps his hands and he looks like he's about to shut down our brainstorming. The thought of adding anything more to our dinner is probably giving him a conniption, but these ideas are too good to stop now. I rush in before he says anything. "I think we should expand the dinner. What if we asked the graphic design kids to make us a flyer and we posted on social media? My friend Angelica would do it."

Someone from the back yells, "Word! We could tag some famous folks. Meek Mill sometimes promotes things like this to his fans, and Joel Embiid might show love."

Chef Ayden looks like he wants to interrupt, but people keep calling out other suggestions and my hand flies over my notebook as I record them all. When the recommendations die down I raise that same hand and wait on Chef Ayden to give me a nod. "As the fund-raising chair, I want to propose we bring our ideas to Principal Holderness. We don't have much time, but the worst that could happen is he says no. Sometimes you have to ask anyway, right?"

Chef gives us a long nod. "I have some friends from my culinary school days and colleagues who might be willing to attend or contribute. It doesn't hurt to ask."

By the time we leave class, I think we're all feeling a bit high. Not only might we raise the money we need, but this is also an opportunity to show off our chops to the school and our families, and possibly the whole city.

To the Bone

The next week zooms by like a train: I move from one thing to the next without stopping and I'm left tired to my very bones. I mean that literally — even my bones need a nap. Between my weekend shifts at the Burger Joint, finishing college applications, creating flyers, using social media to boost the fund-raiser, and mornings cooking for the lunch crowd or afternoons serving them, I never have time to breathe. Even at home, I'm making dinner or washing dishes, and as much as I love cooking, I could use a pause.

And none of that even touches on the fact that I'm usually exhausted just from having to run around ensuring Babygirl is fed and clothed, has been to the park, has been read to, has slept well, is up on her checkups, and is ready for her visits with her father.

There are some nights I want to cry myself to sleep from how much I'm carrying, but even my eyes are too tired to make tears work properly.

Thanksgiving in our house this year is a quiet event. Since I get Babygirl for Christmas, New Year's, and Three Kings' Day, Tyrone and I decided it makes sense for him to take her for Thanksgiving. So this year it's just me and 'Buela eating a small pernil and arroz and rainbow chard, watching the Eagles in an away game.

When my cell phone buzzes I know it's Malachi before I even look at the screen. All of 'Buela's family has already called her, Aunt Sarah called me and we spoke for a few moments, then she promised to send me an email with a pie recipe I requested, and Gelly is caught up with Laura's family so she won't be pressed to reach me.

"Hey, Santi. I just wanted to wish you

a happy Thanksgiving. What'd you make?"

I hesitate before answering. "Chocolate pudding, Malachi. You should try some," I say, my face splitting into a smile.

Winter Dinner

It's the afternoon of Monday, December 9, and Schomburg Charter High School is quiet as the last of the students leave. The only people still in the building are the teachers finalizing their grading, and the custodians setting up tables and chairs in the gym. In about two hours the school will reopen for the public to come enjoy the Winter Dinner. But in our small part of the building, game time is right now.

"All right, class! Tonight is the big night. People have paid money to be here in our fancy gymnasium, and we are almost sold out. The basketball team even rescheduled a game so we could use this space, and Principal Holderness has invited folks from the superintendent's office. Black Thought from the Roots retweeted a post and over a hundred people from the community have bought tickets. We did everything we could to have people show up, but now we have to show out."

It's almost like a mini prom. We've wheeled in the long tables from the cafeteria and covered them with cloth (it turns out Angelica's fabrics did not go to waste!). We have little Christmas lights set up throughout the entranceway to give the room a nice winter-night effect. The basketball hoops have been pushed back and the score screens are covered with the menu printed on large poster paper. And each of us is in our clean uniform, our caps pinned on tight. It's not some swanky rooftop affair, but damn if it ain't good for being a high school gym transformation in less than two weeks.

I tune back in to Chef's speech. "They're ready to be wined and dined. Well not wined, that'd be illegal. Make it good, follow orders. Each group knows what they're in charge of, right? Any menu questions can be directed at Emoni or me. Follow the recipes precisely. I got them down to the last grain of salt." Chef gives me a look.

The whole class nods at Chef. I don't know about anyone else, but it feels like even my butterflies have butterflies in *their* bellies. Next to me, Malachi hums Meek to himself. Without thinking, I take his hand and give it a light squeeze. He squeezes back and my nerves die down a bit. Although now my hand is tingling where we touched. I can't win!

Everyone jumps to their stations and I meet Richard and Amanda at ours. We're in charge of assembling spoonfuls of sweet-potato casserole but with a Spanish twist. That was my idea, a Southern holiday meal meets a twist of southern Spain. Most of the hors d'oeuvres were prepared beforehand so we just need to get them in the oven and put on the finishing garnishes. I begin scooping sweet-potato casserole onto ceramic serving spoons while Richard garnishes them with sugared walnuts and Spanish sausage. Three months ago, most of us had never even tried Spanish cuisine, and today we're hosting a semi-Spanish-themed banquet.

We work like machines. I spoon and pass the bite to my left. Richard adds walnuts and sausage, and passes the plate. Amanda adds parsley and cleans the plate. Chili aioli would make this bomb. A sweet and savory bite. I almost walk to the spice cabinet, then stop myself.

That's not the recipe.

We make trays and trays of food; some are set forward for the students who will begin serving. These are the skewers of winter veggies and single-serve portions of herbed stuffing with jamón ibérico — the less hearty bites. While the first course is being distributed the rest of us begin wiping down our stations. Our mini bites of sweet potato and mac and cheese will be going out next.

The night moves as chaotically and quickly as Angelica when she torpedoes into a room. Before I know it, the last course, individual apple pies, has gone out, and the only thing left to do is to file out and a take a bow.

It feels strange to leave the kitchen. As

if I'm naked. Every recipe that went out had my thumbprint on it, and whether people enjoyed the meal falls on me.

A NUMBERS GAME

Those of us who have been in the kitchen prepping enter the back of the gym and join the rest of our classmates who were serving. Chef Ayden has just been announced and he walks onstage. He wipes his huge hand on his chef's coat before shaking the principal's. Although we are the ones who have been cooking, his coat has just as many puffs of flour and sauce stains as ours do.

"As many of you have been hearing throughout the night, in addition to being our annual Winter Dinner, this meal has also served as a fund-raiser for our Culinary Arts class, which will be traveling to Spain during spring break. They've been working diligently throughout the first two quarters to raise money, and this was their culminating fund-raiser."

Principal Holderness opens an envelope. Richard throws an arm over Amanda's shoulder. I squeeze my hands into fists and hold my breath.

"And the final tally for the evening is . . . two thousand dollars!"

I quickly tally all the amounts from the lunches and auction revenue with tonight's money. At fifteen dollars a ticket we have about two thousand dollars left after we cover the cost of the food. With the new total each individual owes about two hundred seventy-five dollars.

That's more money than I have saved, especially with the balance being due by the end of the week. I blink back the tears in my eyes. *This is a happy moment, Emoni. Something to be proud of. Don't let them see you cry.*

"Please put your hands together for the students who fed you well tonight, Culinary Arts Class Section Three." Principal Holderness gestures to us in the back and at once the dim room is flooded with light so the guests can see us. I squint to adjust my eyes to the light and now I can see the room too. 'Buela sits at one of the front tables, and when everyone stands and claps for us she bounces up and down on the balls of her feet as if she wants to jump. I see Ant and June from the barbershop in their T-shirts and jeans, clapping with enthusiasm. Julio must have reached out to them. Ms. Martinez from next door is nodding as if she knew we'd be able to accomplish this all along. Around the whole room I spot neighbors, block homies, 'Buela's church friends, directors from the cultural center, shop owners, all here to support a dream.

Malachi puts his arm around me and Amanda grabs my hand. "We did this. We fed two hundred and fifty people and showed them why we deserve their time and attention and money," she says.

I nod around the lump in my throat. I don't know how I'll come up with my portion of the money, but I'm glad my ideas made it easier for the rest of the class. And she's right: we made something special happen here tonight.

The night ends soon after that, and although we need to go to the kitchen to finish cleaning up, most of the class is dapping up homies and saying hi to family members. I'm carving a path over to 'Buela when a woman steps in my way.

"Excuse me?" She looks familiar but I can't place her face.

I nod at her. "Can I help you?"

She puts out her hand and when I grasp it her handshake is firm and her palm is rough. "Chef told me to speak to you? Emoni, right?"

I nod at her and let go of her hand. "I'm not sure if you remember me," she says. And the moment she says it, I do remember. She's the chef from the fancy restaurant 'Buela took me to, Café . . . Something?

"After you came to my restaurant I mentioned meeting you to Paul, Chef Ayden, and he could not stop saying how you're a talented chef-in-training. I was happy to accept his invitation here to-night to try your food. He tells me you were in charge of the menu?"

I nod as if none of this is a big deal,

although on the inside I'm a whirl of emotions. For a moment I forget about what money I have left to raise. Chef Ayden was boasting about me? I clear my throat. "Chef Ayden helped me a bit with the menu."

The woman nods. "The food was delicious. I especially liked the bite of sweet-potato casserole."

I smile at her. "If you thought that was good you should try an idea I have of adding chili aioli. The spice will layer well with the sweetness." I realize I'm talking to her as if we are homegirls and immediately blush. I don't want her to think I'm bragging.

She cocks her head at me. "Well, I'd love to try that one day. I wanted to give my compliments to the chef. Here's my card. I think what you all are doing here is remarkable. Have a great time in Spain."

She gives me the small square of cardstock. *Lisa Williams, Owner and Executive Chef, Café Sorrel.*

She gives me a little nod and moves in the direction of Chef Ayden. I stare at the card in my palm. I tuck it into my jacket pocket just as I'm swept up by 'Buela.

She hugs me so hard we rock back and forth. "I'm so proud of you, nena! This is amazing. The food was good and everybody looked happy. They all cleaned their plates. I could taste you in the sweet potato. You made those, right? They tasted like you. Even Baby Emma could tell." I look at the stroller where Babygirl is licking the palm of her hand.

'Buela and I are still rocking on our feet, but she suddenly pulls back. "Oh, I'm being rude. Let me introduce you to someone."

Behind her is a short, skinny man with one of those old-school fedora hats. He has glasses, and a huge mustache, and the sweetest eyes. "This is Joseph Jagoda. He works at Dr. Burke's office. I went there to pass out flyers last week. The office made a donation!" I smile at Mr. Jagoda.

"Thanks so much for supporting us." It seems Julio's grassroots efforts have inspired 'Buela.

Then I'm being hugged up by Angelica, and Julio's barbershop friends each give me daps and pat me on the back.

Babygirl smiles in her stroller and shakes her sticky hand at me. I break away from everyone and pick her up, letting her sweet baby scent ground me. I don't know how I'll get the rest of this money, but I know that I did more for this single day than I ever thought possible, and that's something to be proud of.

Hook, Line, and Sinker

My classmates are all still hyped the next day when we arrive at school. I'm glad that for the first time in a month and a half none of us have early shifts for the rest of the week.

Chef tried to cancel our lunches entirely. He told us he announced it at a staff meeting that after the Winter Dinner he'd be pulling the program, but the other teachers threw a fit, so restaurant lunches will start back up in the new year on Tuesdays and Thursdays. Anyone who shows up early to cook gets extra credit, and anyone who shows up to serve gets to keep their tips. And since I need extra money and extra credit I will be showing up as often as I can.

When we got home after the dinner, I asked 'Buela if she could lend me the money for the trip's final deposit; I'll put in a double shift at the Burger Joint to pay her back. But she told me she'd already spent her last disability check on bills and Christmas gifts for family back home. Not to mention, she donated the night of the Winter Dinner. She offered to return the gifts or ask a friend for help, but the look in her eyes was so sad and ashamed I patted her arm and told her I'd work it out. I thought about asking Julio for it, but when I was telling him about the dinner he cut me off to say that I inspired him and he's sponsoring a holiday block party to raise money for the local school. I knew he'd say educating the undereducated is more important than traveling to Europe, and I wouldn't even be able to argue.

I push these thoughts away as I'm cleaning my station. Malachi comes over and leans his elbows near my burners. "Hey, Santi. I have a hookup to some tickets for the Disney On Ice show this weekend. You wanna go?"

"Since when do you have Philly hookups?"

He smirks. "Is that a yes?"

He's standing close to me and I wonder how he can smell so good when we've been sweating and dealing with food all class. "I don't know, Malachi. I don't really date like that, and this sounds like a date." I wipe my area, making sure not to get too close to my burners or to Malachi — both would probably leave me singed.

"See, that's the thing, though, this wouldn't be a date," he says and smiles wide, showing off all his teeth. "I can get a couple of tickets. You can invite Angelica, her girlfriend, bring little queen Emma. Even your abuela can come if that will get you to say yes."

Dang. Malachi knows just how to get to me. Hooking up my entire family with tickets to something we've always seen in commercials but never in real life puts a lump in my throat. I finish with my station and grab my bag from the cubby. I clear my throat. "That's really nice of you, Malachi. It means a lot to me. I could use some fun. What day?"

"Don't go getting soft on me, Santi." But he doesn't look at me. I think we are both so used to dissing each other that in this moment of sincerity we feel shy. "The tickets are for this Saturday."

"I'll organize my people. You want help cleaning your station? Chef will get angry if he sees you haven't unplugged your burners."

But Malachi waves me off. "Nah, you already made the kid's day."

COMPLICATIONS

I've always had a feeling Malachi was interested. Even if he hasn't said those exact words. And to be honest, even if he *had* said those exact words I probably wouldn't have believed him. If there's one thing I learned from Tyrone, it's that a person can say all kinds of things but it may not be more than that, just speech. Malachi's actions, however, tell me time and again that he's feeling me.

And I don't know what to do about it. It takes me the whole bus ride home to get the courage to bring it up to Angelica, and even then I hide it behind Malachi's invitation.

Angelica is immediately on her phone texting Laura. "Cool, she says she's free so we're both good to go." I'm quiet on the walk to my house. Angelica comes inside with me. She's going to take photographs of a new mural in Port Richmond this afternoon, and there's a thrift store there that offers cash for secondhand clothes. She's offered to sell a bag of old shirts and jeans for me.

We're upstairs in my room, where I'm tossing the clothes into a large plastic bag. I hope I can earn enough to make a dent on what I owe for the trip. I have a ton of Babygirl's clothing that doesn't fit her anymore, and I throw in two brandname shirts I got last Christmas that I hope will sell for a good amount.

"That shirt is cute; why are you giving it away?" she says, grabbing a *Doc McStuffins* shirt from the top of the pile.

"Because it doesn't fit Babygirl. Unless you're having a child sometime soon?" I say, raising an eyebrow at her.

"Oh, yup, that's at the top of Laura's to-do list, get me pregnant."

Angelica plumps up the pillow and leans back on my bed. "So, is this like a double date this weekend?"

"What? No. In fact, he even invited 'Buela and Babygirl."

"Ohhh. That's deep. He's already trying to get in with the family."

I stop what I'm doing. "I think he's serious about going out with me. It's just, you know how I am with boys."

Angelica grabs a shirt from my hands and folds it. "You are scared of being hurt, girl. And you never think you have time for yourself."

I shake my head. "I *don't* have time for myself. And I don't have time for boys."

Angelica and I fold silently side by side. When the bag is full she ties it up tight and I walk her downstairs. At the doorway she pauses. "Maybe it's not about time, Emoni. Maybe it's about having things on your terms. Being with Malachi? It doesn't have to look like anything except what you two make it. And if anyone can take ingredients that shouldn't work and make something delicious out of them, it's you. Give my goddaughter a hug from me."

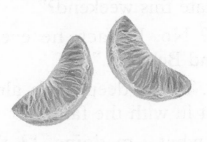

PRIDE

It's Wednesday — two days left before the money is due. I finally swallow my pride and approach Chef Ayden. "Chef Ayden, I was wondering if I could speak with you?"

Chef Ayden looks at me with a grin. Ever since the Winter Dinner, Chef's been smiling more, giving people high fives. I know he feels relief that the majority of the money was covered. A relief I do not feel.

Angelica was able to sell my clothes for forty-five dollars. 'Buela left a big-faced fifty near my bed this morning, and I'm not sure where she got it; her disability check doesn't come again until next month. But that still means I have two days to find a hundred and eighty dollars.

"Emoni, the fund-raiser of the century. What can I do for you?"

I smile back at him although I feel sick inside. How can you be a good fund-raiser if you didn't reach your goal? "I was wondering if I could maybe get a bit more time to pay the deposit? I'm still short some." I slide the hundred dollars his way. He looks down at the bills then up at me.

"Oh, Emoni. I wish I'd known you needed assistance. We had some students ask for help early on and we were able to figure out a payment plan, and even some extensions, but it's a bit late to scramble and make changes. . . . I'll have to talk to Principal Holderness."

But I can tell from his face he isn't optimistic.

"Does this mean if I can't find the money, I can't go?"

He slides the bills over to me, then pats my hand. "Of course you're going, even I have to pay for it myself," he says. But the look in his eye is the same as 'Buela's when she told me she didn't have the cash. Two days just isn't enough time for people to rearrange their holiday money for something that isn't a necessity. He pats my hand again. "We just have to come up with a creative solution. I'll talk to Principal Holderness. Hold on to your money for now."

Thursday morning I wake up and everything in my body wants to stay in bed. I want to hide under my blankets and pretend the world doesn't exist outside these walls. But Babygirl wakes out of a dream screaming and I pick her up to soothe her. It takes fifteen minutes to get her calm enough to dress and feed, and I know I won't have time to dress myself in anything other than the leggings and T-shirt I slept in. When 'Buela asks me something about washing the dishes I almost bite her head off, I'm in such a bad mood, but I catch myself before I say something I'll regret. If I can't go on this trip it's no one's fault, especially not 'Buela's.

Angelica must be able to tell how I'm feeling because she pulls her arm through mine as we walk to the bus stop and tries to distract me with celebrity gossip. When we are finally on the bus, I use my phone as a way to hide my face from her. I don't want her to see the tears in my eyes. I check my email and there seems to be a message from Aunt Sarah — her name is in the subject line — but it's a different address than the one I'm used to seeing; almost as if it was rerouted from a website.

I open the email and the first thing I see is a dollar amount:

$300
Note: Hey, niece. Sorry this is late. I know you told me in your last email the fund-raiser would end earlier this week. I pooled this together from all your other aunties and uncles and cousins; I hope you can still use it. I loved the pictures you sent from the dinner. I've never been anywhere farther than Raleigh, but I gather everyone needs some pocket change when they leave home, right?

We are all so proud of you. Nya

would be proud of you, too.

Love,
Aunt Sarah & the Family

I'm shocked, and it must be visible because Angelica grabs my arm.

"Emoni, what's wrong? You're trembling."

Aunt Sarah is my email auntie, the strongest connection to my mother, my kitchen confidante, but she's never sent money before, never organized that side of the family to send me a gift. I look out the window at the clouds parting in the same way my bad mood is, sunlight peeking through both, and I know for a fact there's more than one kind of magic in this world.

On Ice

I've seen commercials for Disney On Ice my whole life but never thought about going. And still, as we wait in line outside the Wells Fargo Center, I feel as giddy as the little kids jumping up and down in anticipation. From her stroller, Babygirl keeps pointing at everyone and everything. Laura and Angelica hold hands, trying to look all cool and like they're only here because I asked, but I know they're excited, too. Malachi is the funniest of us all, bouncing up and down on his toes to see if we're moving closer to the front of the line, making goofy faces at Babygirl, and asking every Disney character who walks past us for a picture. 'Buela declined his invitation and said she was going to meet up with a friend instead. "You young people go have fun with your Disney. I'm going to drink a cafecito and gossip."

As we approach the entrance, Malachi fishes out the tickets from his pocket and steps forward. Angelica reaches down to fuss with the cover of Babygirl's stroller. "I been meaning to ask you, how did Tyrone take this news?"

I don't look at her when I shrug, and she shoves my shoulder.

"Emoni, please tell me you told him," she hisses at me, but I don't have a chance to say anything — not that I was going to say a damn thing — before Malachi is ushering the rest of us forward.

But Angelica won't quit. She whispers low enough so that only I can hear her. "Emoni, didn't he lose his shit last time because Babygirl was in the same house as Malachi?"

I pull her closer to me and make sure Malachi and Laura are speaking with each other before I say anything. "Angelica, he flipped out last time because he didn't like the idea of me dating. I know he has Babygirl around other girls. I know he dates. It's not his weekend, and if I want to take my daughter to Disney On Ice, who is he to say I can't?"

Angelica shakes her head and throws up her hands. Laura must sense her girl being all dramatic because she stops mid-sentence to look at us. Both Angelica and I paste smiles on our faces.

"Everything okay?" Malachi asks when we catch up with them. I smile bigger, too big. He's got to know something is bugging me, but I'm not going to let Angelica's words water the seed of guilt blooming in my stomach.

"Everything is fine. Thank you for this. I know Emma is going to love it. Right, Babygirl?" At both of our faces peering down at her, Emma gets shy and bur-rows her head into the side of her stroller. I laugh. "Trust me, she's excited. That's her excited face."

Malachi laughs. "Cool. I'm glad this worked out. My aunt gets extra tickets and she sees it every year."

"Your aunt?" I say. We are finally at the gate. "I thought you said you had a 'friend' with a hookup?"

"I never said 'friend.' My aunt works

here. She's my hookup. We're actually
about to see her now. Smile, Santi."

SIDE BY SIDE

"Hey, Auntie Jordyn." Malachi leans down to hug a little woman in a black collared shirt and slacks. The woman has a walkie-talkie in one hand, which she pats against Malachi's back when he bends down to hug her. She still has her arm around his waist when she turns to the group. He points at each of us in turn. "Let me introduce you to Angelica and Laura. And that's Emoni. And the little queen in the stroller is Emma."

Auntie Jordyn looks up at him with a gruff expression. "Boy, what did I tell you about pointing at people? Just because your momma isn't here doesn't mean you forget what she's taught you!" But as quick as she frowned she's smiling and letting Malachi go. "And this little one, well, isn't she precious? I'm glad these tickets could go to good use. With my kids out the house so long, my complimentary tickets usually go unused. I'm glad this year someone who can actually appreciate it will be watching." She pats Malachi on the cheek and I instantly love her. Malachi's smile is clearly inherited from his mom's side because the woman looks just as happy and sweet as he does when he smiles.

"Thank you, ma'am. We're really looking forward to it," I say.

She gives me a look that I don't know how to read. "Malachi talks about you all the time. I'm glad to finally meet you."

I don't look at Malachi as I nod.

"Well, you all go on in. I have some paperwork to do in my office, so I won't be able to join you. But make sure you enjoy!" We enter through one of the first-floor gates and look for the letter-and-number combination that indicates our row. As I replay the conversation something twists in my stomach. Malachi talks about me to his aunt?

Before I know it, my thoughts are

absorbed in the music, the colorful lights, the characters in their large costumes as they skate and twirl and jump in the air. I don't have any words except to say it's magical. And I'm just as into it as Baby-girl. She bounces along in my lap and Angelica's lap, clapping and pointing. I wish I could do this for her more often, give her these kinds of adventures.

Malachi leans over, his breath warm on my ear. "Smile, Santi. This is the greatest show on earth."

"You got the wrong show, homie. I think that saying was for a circus show, not Disney."

"I wasn't talking about what's happening over there," Malachi says, tugging on one of my curls. "I was talking about what's happening right here." He links his fingers with mine, and I'm glad Baby-girl is in Angelica's lap, bouncing and bucking. I'm so glad my hand is free so it can be inside of Malachi's.

"You're ridiculous," I say, laughing. "What does that even mean?"

Malachi doesn't answer. And I don't pull my hand from his for the rest of the show.

CHIVALRY

Auntie Jordyn lets us out through a side door, which means we avoid the rush. We are immediately sucker-punched by cold air and I pull the plastic cover tighter over Emma's stroller. One of the things that I hate most about winter is that even though it's only four thirty, it's already dark out, and the temperature dropped twenty degrees in the two hours we were inside so now it's barely in the double digits.

I try to blow heat onto my gloved hands. Malachi is still inside speaking with his aunt. Laura and Angelica are snuggling into each other's necks. "You two go ahead. Laura's house is in the opposite direction so it's not like we're walking to the same train." Angelica gives me exactly three seconds to reconsider before she grabs Laura's hand and flounces, literally *flounces,* away with Laura laughing behind her.

"Goodbye, Emoni. Thanks for including us," Laura says over her shoulder. I don't blame them for not wanting to stick around. I like how light Laura makes Angelica feel, how happy they are to hold hands and just love.

And then Malachi is standing beside me, and he's tucked my hand into his, and he's holding the stroller with his other hand, and I'm a web of knots. The feelings of this growing crush tangle with the feelings of guilt and doubt about whether or not I should pursue this. But I wish I could strip myself of my past and enjoy who I am right now.

"My aunt ordered us a ride-share so we don't have to walk in the cold when we get off at your bus stop." So that's what they'd been in there discussing — where I lived.

"I don't have a car seat for her so I'm

not sure that will work," I say.

But Malachi surprises me. "I know. We requested a car with a car seat." It's not the kind of thing I would imagine him thinking about.

We are quiet as we wait, and when the car pulls up I unbuckle Babygirl and Malachi holds open the door for me before folding up her stroller. We ride the twenty minutes home in silence, listening to R&B on the radio. My house is dark when we walk in. I close the door behind me and turn on the living room light. I'm so glad Disney tired Babygirl out and she was asleep in the car before the first song finished playing on the radio. It's too early for her to go to bed, but I don't have it in my heart to wake her up. I'll just deal with her midnight energy when it comes. I take her upstairs and lay her down in her crib. When I come back down Malachi is using the bathroom.

I'm rinsing out a glass in the sink when I hear him follow me into the kitchen. I turn to ask him if he wants some water, but his arm that's slipped around my waist and touching bare skin startles me. I freeze for a moment, and it's not until I hear the glass shatter against the tile floor that I realize it fell from my hand.

We scramble back from each other and I listen to Babygirl's monitor to make sure the noise didn't wake her. When I'm greeted by silence from Babygirl, I drop to my knees to pick up the shards of glass. Malachi follows me down and we are nose to nose for one second before I scoop up some big chunks and carry them to the trash bin. Malachi grabs the broom in the kitchen corner and takes care of the smaller pieces.

"You're good with kids," I say when we've cleaned up.

"Yeah, my mom used to say the same thing. Even when he was being an asshole I had patience with my little brother. Emoni, are you bleeding?"

I look down at my hand. I hadn't even noticed the small cut on my palm.

"Let me see," he says. He pulls me over to the sink and puts my hand under running water, then inspects my cut palm. After a moment, he curls my hands around his and kisses my knuckles.

"Not so bad. Nothing a little peroxide

and a Band-Aid won't fix."

I shake my head. "Dr. Malachi Johnson, here to save the day." He applied to Morehouse early decision weeks ago and should be hearing back any day now.

"Not yet. But that's the plan." Malachi and I have talked about his dream to start a practice back in his hood. He insists they need more people from home trying to help home, and I think about the way he cradled my hand and inspected my cut; how he makes me smile when I'm upset. I think about how sure he is when he walks into a room and how he participates in every class he takes, and I know Malachi is going to be an amazing doctor one day. Sometimes, when he talks about returning to Newark, he reminds me of my father; a love for home so deep you go out into the world with the sole purpose of bringing the world back to your hood. And the similarities make me smile and hurt at the same time. Malachi has his future planned out. He knows exactly what he wants and how he's going to get it. And me? I've barely finished my college essay, much less submitted it anywhere.

Malachi awkwardly shuffles his feet. I take my hand out of his. I want to hold my own hand when I ask the question.

"Malachi, what is this? What are we doing?"

He takes a step back. "I don't know. I don't think that's a question I need to answer by myself, is it? You seemed to want to take it slow so we've been taking it slow."

I remember what Angelica said the last time she was here. About designing my own kind of reality. And I think part of that is owning when I don't know what I want that reality to look like.

"Thank you for taking it slow. To be honest, I'm not sure what I want. Not with you, not with college, not with anything. Babygirl is the only thing in my life I'm clear on." It costs me to say the words; I feel like I'm giving him a picture of all the different questions I have, of how much of a mess I am. But instead of stepping back and saying I'm right, Malachi takes my uncut hand in his. And even though I didn't think I wanted him to hold it a second ago, I'm glad we are touching again. He doesn't say a word. And somehow the silence lets me push more words out.

"I think I like you." Each word is a small piece of myself I hand over. "And I want to keep doing this. Being friends. Who like each other. Not that you've said you like me."

Malachi gives my fingers a squeeze and smiles. Not his full dimple smile, but a smile that seems like it's just for me. "You need to hear me say it, huh? I like you."

I gulp. "I don't want to disappoint you. I don't know . . ." What I don't know is what to say next. My hand is still in his and this moment feels too awkward. I'm not used to asking for anything. "I don't know what I want from you. Or if I want anything more than this. I don't know if or when I'll be ready for more than this." There. I said it.

But maybe I didn't say it, because Malachi seems confused. "Emoni, are we talking about sex?"

I try to tug my hand out of his but he holds mine fast. "I just don't know if I'm ready for that. Or to be your girlfriend. Or anything more than this." I can't stop

322

repeating myself but it's like the words have dried up and all I have left in the bottom of my cup are the same phrases I've been saying.

He shrugs. "Okay."

"Okay?"

"We'll figure it out, right? And if one of us needs something different, we'll say that. Right?"

He leans down and for a second I think he's going to kiss me, but then he just rests his forehead against mine. This can't be real life.

"I think I'm going to head home. It sounds like Babygirl might be waking up upstairs." And I realize he's right. Babygirl is babbling from her crib.

"Are you going to call a car again?" I ask.

"Nah, I'll walk to the train," he says, zipping up his coat and pulling his hat down tight over his ears.

"That's, like, a twenty-minute walk. In the cold."

And then the dimples are back. "I know. I think it'll do me some good."

I walk him to the door. And just as he leaves he turns back one more time. "Did you hear the last song that played in the car on our way here?"

Of course I did. I was even singing along; the Roots are legends and that song is a classic. I nod.

"Don't worry, Emoni. You got me."

When It Rains

With only three days left of school before winter break, things have been busy. Angelica has been spending her lunch periods working on a final project for her Graphic Design class. Malachi has been using all his free time applying for scholarships. And me? I've been holed up in the school library studying for these last exams before the quarter finishes.

It's probably because I'm so distracted that I break the one rule every student at Schomburg Charter knows better than to break: I get caught on my phone in between classes. I was trying to call 'Buela after lunch to remind her I was going grocery shopping today, and the next thing I know, a guard has plucked it out of my hand and is already writing me up. I try to explain but he won't budge.

The guard is new, and I know he doesn't know me or my circumstances because all he can do is remind me of the same tired rules. "If you want your phone back, you'll need a signed release form from your parent or guardian."

And I almost laugh in his face when he utters those words. I can sign permission slips for my own daughter but can't sign one for myself.

"Sir, I really think you should speak to my advisor. I have a kid. I need my phone."

But either he doesn't believe me or he doesn't care because he just shrugs and leaves with my phone in his hand. I could go to the front office and try and get someone there on my side, but I know from past experience the office staff usually sides with the security officers. I'll have to wait until the morning to get my phone back. By the time the end of my day arrives I'm ready to be home.

I bump the door open with my hip and readjust the two grocery bags I got after school. " 'Buela? Babygirl?" I call upstairs as I go into the kitchen and set the bags onto the counter. I sure hope 'Buela didn't have another doctor's appointment today, but she would have brought Babygirl home first. I plan to sit her down tonight and ask what's happening. I've been watching her closely, and even changed up what I've been cooking for her to include more vegetables and less butter, but I know that all these doctor's appointments must mean something is wrong, and I'm going to have to face it sooner or later regardless of how much she wants to protect me. Maybe they are upstairs taking a nap.

I try to distract myself from thoughts of illness by putting away the groceries. I might have gone a little overboard today buying some new spices — I swear I can spend all day at the supermarket. I especially love the one in our neighborhood that brings in ingredients straight from the island. I get to walk the aisles and pick up herbs and peppers from all over the world, thinking of all the ways to remix my favorite dishes.

" 'Buela?" I call out again, but nobody answers. It's almost four thirty and it's strange for the house to be so quiet at this time. I walk through the living room, picking up toys and bibs. I call out again and it only takes my going halfway up the stairs to realize no one is home. The upstairs is dark and silent. 'Buela must have taken Babygirl to the park, although it's too cold for that. Maybe she got caught up talking to one of our neighbors. I hope she didn't forget she asked me to do the grocery shopping — the last thing we need is for her to walk in here with more gallons of milk or extra boxes of cereal. I organize the magazines in the living room, wipe down the coffee table, and put away all of Babygirl's toys and books that somehow always wind up between the couch cushions like a sharp gift for my backside when I sit down. I glance at the wall clock, almost five. The sky outside has already lost the sun. 'Buela doesn't have *that* many friends in the neighborhood. She's mostly friendly with the neighborhood church ladies and the families on either side of our house, but not enough to drop by their houses.

Something is wrong. And as if it guessed my thoughts, the house phone rings. I dive for it.

"Hello?" I bite back on the panic I feel.

A throat clears. "Emoni? This is Mrs. Palmer. Tyrone's mother."

Close to three years and she still thinks I don't know her relationship to my family. "Hello, Mrs. Palmer. Is everything okay?"

The phone rattles some before she speaks again. "Well, no. Everything is not okay. Emma came down with a fever. The daycare has been trying to call you all day, but no one has answered. They tried your grandmother's cell phone but it seems to be off and no one was answering the house phone."

Damn, damn, damn. "Is Emma okay? Where is she? My phone . . . is still at school. Do you have her?"

"Mm-hmm," Mrs. Palmer says, as if she doubts my explanation and believes I would intentionally not answer my phone. "Well, it's a good thing they had *both* parents on file. They eventually called Tyrone, who called me. I left work early to pick the baby up. Doesn't your grandmother usually do this? Where is she? I'd like to speak to her."

Mrs. Palmer always does this. Acts as if I'm too young and stupid to discuss my own daughter. But the thing is, I don't know where 'Buela is, but I don't want Mrs. Palmer to think that both 'Buela and I are irresponsible. "She had a doctor's appointment and she's not home yet. It must have run late. She's always good about picking her up. Are you home? I'll come get Babygirl." I'm frantic to get my baby in my arms but I bite out some politeness. "I'm sorry they bothered you, Mrs. Palmer."

"Yes, well. Now that I know you're home, I'll drop her off myself. There's a reason we got that baby seat installed, after all."

I hang up the phone. My bottom lip hurts and I realize I've been chewing on it the whole conversation. I throw a scarf on and head outside to wait for Mrs. Palmer.

IT POURS

Mrs. Palmer's brown suede coat sways over her heavyset frame as she undoes all the buckles that hold Babygirl safe in the car. I try not to anxiously peer past the car door or push her and undo Babygirl myself. I tug the scarf around my neck to keep Mrs. Palmer from seeing my hands are trembling.

Mrs. Palmer plucks Babygirl from her car seat and backs out of the car. She'd be a pretty woman if she didn't always have her face looking like she smelled something ripe. She didn't like me from jump, since before I was pregnant, but Tyrone said she's like that with everyone. She hands Babygirl over carefully and the gentle way she does it makes me almost like her.

I rub my head against the top of Baby-girl's soft hair. She whimpers up at me, and even through the crown of hair I can feel how warm she is. I murmur to her a bit before tucking her to me. I'm small, but never too small to carry my kid like she's the most precious thing I have. From the trunk of the car Mrs. Palmer pulls out Babygirl's stroller and diaper bag.

"Thank you, Mrs. Palmer. I appreciate it. Again, I'm sorry about this."

She clears her throat and gives a brisk nod. "Well, I certainly won't be dropping work every time you and your grand-mother are too negligent to take care of Emma. I know you and Tyrone have an informal arrangement, and I would be remiss if I didn't say that so far it seems to be working for you two, but you best believe that if he ever chooses to chal-lenge that arrangement in court, I will ensure this incident is put on the record."

The polite smile slides off my face. Did Mrs. Palmer just hint at Tyrone wanting custody of Babygirl? Did she just imply she would be supportive of that, even though she's never actually wanted Babygirl? I place my trembling hand on my child's hot cheek to keep it from doing harm to Mrs. Palmer.

"Hey, Babygirl —"

"I really wish you would start calling her by her name. All this 'Babygirl' mess is likely to confuse her."

I ignore the shit out of Mrs. Palmer because if I said anything right now it would probably burn a permanent hole right through her higher-than-mighty attitude. And I have to remember this is my daughter's grandmother. "Babygirl, I've got you now. Gonna get some medicine in you and make you feel better," I say firmly, kissing the top of her head. I put a hand on her cheek. Besides her whimpers, she's unbelievably quiet. "Goodbye, Mrs. Palmer." I tug the baby bag over my shoulder and drag the stroller with me toward the house steps.

"Wait a second. I picked this up figuring you might not have any — and a little more never hurts if you do."

She hands over a brown paper bag. I peek inside. Children's Tylenol. I grab it with the same hand holding Babygirl.

"For the fever. And really, you should be more responsible about your cell phone. You have a child, Emoni. People need to contact you about her." She hesitates a second, then runs two fingers down Babygirl's cheek. She wiggles those fingers through the air as a goodbye and walks back to her car. She's off before I can wave back. Before I can say thank you. Before I can say I always have plenty of Children's Tylenol. Before I can ask her why Tyrone wasn't the one to pick up Babygirl, or why I'm accused of being the irresponsible one but he's so often excused from having to be as much of a father as I am a mother.

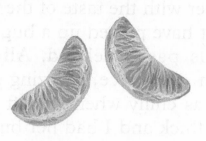

BLOOD BOIL

"Crazy-ass woman. Thinks just because she's an insurance officer at some hospital she can treat me like I'm an idiot." Mrs. Palmer always makes my blood hot. It's like she's a wooly mammoth whose most comfortable seat is my last nerve. Even after all this time, I feel inadequate anytime I speak to her.

Where is 'Buela? She always knows how to smile at Mrs. Palmer, and nod, and pleasantly still get her way. For a moment I'm mad at 'Buela. If she had picked Babygirl up like she was supposed to, this wouldn't have happened. But then I have to remember 'Buela isn't Babygirl's mom.

I sit Babygirl in her booster seat and pour some fresh juice into her sippy cup to help her with the taste of the medicine. She must have picked up a bug at the ice show this past weekend. All of those people in one space, sneezing and stuff. And it was chilly when we left. Her coat is pretty thick and I had her bundled up, but maybe she was just out too long. I need to put towels around the window or call the landlord to turn the heat up higher.

The door snaps open and 'Buela bustles in with her cheeks pink from the cold and mouth red as if she'd been rubbing it. She stops at the door of the kitchen. She has grocery bags in each hand. She must have done rollers late last night because her hair falls in soft waves around her face. She looks pretty, her eyes twinkling.

And the moment I see her I start to cry.

Not even angry, silent tears, but straight-up chest-heaving, face-uglying, snot-immediately-dribbling-into-mouth crying. I put Babygirl's sippy cup on the counter with a trembling hand and wipe my face.

Her bags fall to the floor but I don't see them land because I'm covering my eyes trying to push the tears back in.

"Emoni! ¿Qué te pasa?" 'Buela pulls me to her. "What's wrong?" She holds on to my wrists and tries to peer into my face until I drop my hands and let them hang limp at my side.

"Where . . . were . . . you?" I finally get out through my sobs.

"I had a doctor's appointment, m'ija, and they needed to reschedule it a bit later." She lets me go and walks to the fridge. "I left you a note." She holds up a bit of paper that she'd attached to the fridge with an alphabet magnet.

" 'Buela, you asked me to pick up groceries." She looks at me blankly, the smile falling from her face. "I didn't get home until four thirty. Babygirl has a fever and they were calling from the daycare. They said your phone was turned off. Why would you leave a note on the fridge but not text me?"

She glares at me. "I *did* text you." 'Buela rushes past me and runs upstairs. When she comes back down she holds two little pink socks she slides on Babygirl's feet. She then picks her up and cuddles her close, tight under her chin. "We need to force her to break the fever.

Did you give her medicine?"

"Yeah, Mrs. Palmer bought some Children's Tylenol. And she was nasty to me as usual and she said I was irresponsible and talked about custody and I didn't know where you were."

'Buela's mouth becomes a hard, white line. "You called Mrs. Palmer? And she said what about custody?"

I sniffle back the tears. "No, the daycare called Tyrone. Tyrone called his mother. They didn't know who else to contact. And I think she was just being mean, not serious, but she did mention something about my being unfit."

We stand there unmoving. Unblinking. Babygirl breaks the silence with a sniffle, her little face scrunched up into a red and silent cry. 'Buela reaches for her, but I get there first and pull Babygirl out of her grasp. "It's okay, baby. I'm here. Mommy's here."

I begin to carry her out of the room but turn around before walking through the doorway. " 'Buela, why have you been going to the doctor so much?" I raise myself to my full height. I can take whatever she throws at me.

338

'Buela fiddles with her wedding band before looking at me. "I'm not sick, Emoni. I've lied to you. I haven't had all those doctor's appointments. I just needed a private afternoon with my thoughts where I'm not in this house. Where I'm Gloria again, and not only 'Buela. I don't know how to explain it. And I don't want to talk about it."

I bury my face into Babygirl's neck so neither one of them can see the tears in my eyes, the relief laced with hurt.

HOLIDAYS

'Buela always treated Christmas like she would if she was still on the island, which means that Christmas Eve was a huge deal. A big-ass pernil dinner and coquito, and I got to stay up late and open my gifts at midnight. Then, on Christmas Day I would go to Angelica's house and have Christmas dinner with them and watch holiday specials on TV. It was the best of both worlds. And with Babygirl I try to bring in both traditions, feed her both days, let her open gifts both days. Thankfully she's over her cold and able to enjoy the holiday. And although I'm too old to ask for gifts or expect much, I never know how to react when people get me a gift.

Angelica has me open an elaborately wrapped box, and inside is a really pretty wrap dress that she found at the thrift store and said made her think of me. It's a beautiful dark red and the skirt swirls around my knees. I feel older. Like the woman I always say I am. I baked her a dozen colorful macarons. It took me forever to get them right, but when Angelica opens the bakery box and sees the orange, blue, and pink desserts, I'm glad I kept trying batch after batch. She pulls one out of the box like it's a piece of expensive jewelry. Then she stuffs the whole thing in her mouth and grins, her teeth covered in spun sugar.

On Christmas morning, my cell phone vibrates and I wake up to Malachi, his deep voice breaking on the high notes of a Christmas carol, and it's so silly but also beautiful. I just cradle the phone and wonder at the different kinds of gifts we can give one another.

'Buela and I have been quietly tiptoe-ing around each other since the day Babygirl came home sick, but the holiday throws open the curtains and lets light diminish, or at least hide, the remnants of our awkward conversation.

On New Year's Eve I send Aunt Sarah a picture of her black-eyed peas recipe. I simmered them in a compote of purple grapes, which is not a part of Aunt Sarah's original recipe, but 'Buela says eating grapes at midnight means good fortune for the new year, and in her notes, Aunt Sarah said the same for black-eyed peas. So I figured combining both would double my luck in this coming year.

The rest of my break is fine. I spend a lot of it working afternoons at the Burger Joint, finishing homework assignments due after the break, snapping pictures of Babygirl, and cuddling with her on the couch. I finished my Common App college essay just in time to meet most of the deadlines on January 1. I applied to all the schools that Ms. Fuentes and I discussed, but my heart isn't into them, not even Drexel and its dope culinary arts program. The closer we get to graduation, the more I feel like I want to be *doing,* not spending four years pretending to do.

NEW YEAR, NEW RECIPES

It's my first day back at school after the break, and during Culinary Arts, Chef Ayden gives us our final itinerary for the trip.

At work, I knock softly on the manager's door. Steve doesn't like being "loudly interrupted."

"Steve? It's Emoni. May I speak with you? Please."

"Enter," he calls through the door, like he's some sort of king in *Game of Thrones*. He already sounds annoyed. I push the door open and peek my head in. I try not to roll my eyes. Although he's quick to close the screen he's looking at on the computer, a tab stays open for his social media. Clearly, he's getting a lot of work done. "What can I do for you, Emoni? I hope this isn't another schedule change."

Even though Steve has an empty chair across from his desk, I stay standing. I clear my throat and look around at the chipped-paint walls and corners cluttered with boxes. Everywhere but at Steve. "Kind of. I was hoping —"

He slaps a hand on his desk. "I hope you aren't going to ask me for another favor. I already make too many concessions for you as it is. You need to be home early on school nights. You can only work afternoon on Saturdays because you have to get your daughter ready for . . . something. You can't work Sundays because you need to help your grandmother. It's always an excuse with you. I'm trying to run a business here, Emoni. Not an extracurricular training program for struggling moms."

I swallow hard. It won't help to chew him out. I let go of a long breath. "Of course, Steve. I understand that. I appreciate the exceptions. I know how much work you do to make sure all of your student employees can balance both

344

their jobs and school." Steve likes it when you kiss his ass and if that's what I have to do, fine. I can tell it works because he stops sitting so stiff and uncrosses his arms. He places them on the table with a long, dramatic sigh.

"Fine, what is it this time?"

I step closer to his desk and keep an equal balance of calmness and perkiness, although what I really feel is irritated I have to grovel at all. "I got an opportunity at school to go on a trip to Spain. During my spring break at the end of March. It'll be a week long and I know you usually schedule me for three days a week, but maybe I can work six days the following week when I get back? It's not for a couple of months but I wanted to ask in advance so I can add any hours I might need to balance it. And I worked a lot during the holidays."

Steve leans back in his chair. "This trip sounds like a vacation. You already used vacation days before Christmas. What was that for? Taking your daughter ice-skating or something? Those holiday days you worked were already making up for previous hours."

That was not what we agreed at the time but I don't think correcting Steve will help right now. Steve keeps talking before he lets me answer any of his questions. "Emoni, I want to help. I really do, but aren't you a senior? You probably won't be here next year anyway. Maybe it's time we start looking at other options?"

My heart stops for a second. It sounds like he's trying to fire me. "Am I fired because I asked you for time off? Several months in advance? Even though I'm willing to work the days the following week?"

"No, no. Of course not." Steve sits up straight and holds his hands out, like an alien coming in peace. "I was merely making a suggestion that since it doesn't seem like you can fulfill the hours required for this job that we . . . start considering alternatives."

And I know what he's not saying. I've seen him do it to other employees: he cuts their hours until it costs more money to get to work than you make at work. I nod. "Let's keep it all the way real, Steve. You're cutting my hours?"

Steve folds his hands. "I'm just going to look for other workers to help you balance the hours you can't work." He doesn't look at me when he says it, but I lean over the desk and force his eyes my way when I reply.

"You're a nice man, Steve. So kind. I'm going to tell my grandmother to pray for you." And I hope he can see in my face that I just sprinkled the juju of a spiteful Puerto Rican grandmother all over his life.

MONEY TALKS

Abuelo died before I was born. And he worked a job with little benefits, and definitely no life insurance or any of that. But luckily, by then my father was full-grown and the only mouth 'Buela had to feed was her own. That is, until she adopted me and also realized that her son wouldn't be helping much with my parenting.

When she injured her hand and began receiving disability, money around the house got a lot tighter. The disability check she gets only goes so far, and although she still does small sewing jobs for the church or our neighbors, it takes her three times as long as it used to to get anything done, because her hand begins to ache. Her stitches, slow as they are, are still precise as ever. And she says even though it was her dominant hand that got stuck in the machine, she's thankful it wasn't the hand with her wedding band that's all scarred up.

But once I got pregnant with Babygirl, it quickly became clear that her disability money and side-hustle jobs were going to barely be enough to cover rent and feed the three of us. I've known since I was little that we had to learn to treat money like a rubber band and stretch that jawn until it almost snaps. As soon as I was able to get a work permit in eighth grade, I did. I worked summer jobs, I worked after school, I've always worked to help 'Buela around the house.

And losing my hours at the Burger Joint means I have to find a new way to help, and not just for the rest of this year.

FLASH

January and February move fast as we prepare for state tests, begin work on our final projects, and give one last push to get our grades up before it gets too close to the end of the year. Before I know it, March rolls around.

I should be happy. In three and a half weeks, I'm actually going to Spain, but the first week in March finds me anxious. Steve reduced my hours to two or three a week, and the money I was making wasn't enough to make a dent on most of the costs we have. I finally quit when I realized it wasn't worth the round-trip fare when I was mostly breaking even.

Malachi and I are still circling each other. Friends who hold hands and sometimes flirt, but nothing more. We don't talk about the future and we don't push for more than this. He found out he was accepted to Morehouse back in December, and regardless of what I end up doing there will be distance between us. Angelica has been busy with Laura and some last-minute applications. And the icing on the cake: Tyrone is taking Babygirl this weekend and I can't even look forward to hanging out with her.

When I hand her over to him Saturday morning, the fist around my heart squeezes tight and it takes everything inside me to not ask him if we could skip this weekend. Tyrone bundles her up, and she waves goodbye to me while jibber-jabbering in his ear. I turn in to a hug from 'Buela and she pats my hair.

"Want me to make lunch and then we can watch *Remember the Titans* or *The Blind Spot*?" 'Buela loves a good sports pep talk and I know it's an offer she can't refuse.

'Buela doesn't look at me as she walks to the coat closet and pulls out her long overcoat. The weather is still cold and it might even snow. She wraps a Super Bowl scarf around her neck.

"I can't, m'ija." She doesn't say anything else. I haven't asked about where she goes when she says she's going to a doctor's appointment, even though we both know it's code for "Gloria Time." She's made it clear it isn't my business.

She gives me a kiss on the cheek, and with a final whiff in the air of her vanilla perfume, she shuts the door behind her.

I think about calling Malachi, or seeing if I can bribe Angelica with food, even if it means I crash a date between her and Laura. But instead, I go into the kitchen and take ingredients out of the fridge. I make 'Buela's recipe for sofrito that I'll use to season the ground beef. Softening the garlic and onions, adding tomato paste. This is the first step for most traditional dishes, the flavoring that gives a rich taste for everything from beans to stew. Then I brown meat and make a homemade sauce from fresh tomatoes. I grate fine shreds of mozzarella cheese and boil sheets of pasta. While the oven is preheating, I slowly layer my guilt, my hope, and a hundred dreams. I don't know if it means anything at all, but 'Buela has always said my hands are magical, and I use them now to put all my feelings into the pan. I put together a salad, making sure it's not overdressed, and then I sit down. Watching as the oven timer counts down.

When the oven chimes, I pull the lasagna out and wash the dishes in the sink while I let it rest for a couple of minutes. My fingers are itching to grab my phone, to talk to someone, to distract myself on social media, but instead I take out a plate and place a thick square of lasagna on it, decorating it with some basil. I plate my salad, and set the small kitchen table. From the fridge I pour myself a small glass of 'Buela's holiday wine. I know she'll raise an eyebrow when she sees I had some, but she won't reprimand me; growing up, she was allowed to drink from the time she was fourteen and she finds the alcohol rules on the mainland excessive. And even if she did have something to say, I don't think it would bother me.

Because today I am alone, in my kitchen, with a meal I made myself. I sit at the table and cut a bite of the lasagna. I don't know what I am going to be, or who I am not; my own desires are thickly layered like the food on my plate, but I know that one day soon I'll be a grown-ass woman. So, I let myself enjoy the meal, the moment, and my own company.

SPAIN

"Are you sure you have everything?"

"Sí, 'Buela," I answer for the fiftieth time. It's finally the day I leave for Spain, and my suitcase is packed, Babygirl's daycare pickup schedule has been finalized by 'Buela and Mrs. Palmer, and we've agreed repeatedly that I'll Face-Time them every night.

"Did you pack a skirt for church?" I nod. Even though she and I both know I'm not going to church unless it's part of a tourist event.

'Buela peers into my suitcase. "And you put all your hair product in Ziploc baggies? The worst thing would be if they

355

spill all over your clothes."

I can imagine several worse things, but I nod dutifully. "Sí, 'Buela."

She claps her hands together. "Oh! An umbrella, what if it rains?" I grab her arm before she finds something else for me to pack. And I hug her tight. "It's only seven days. I'm going to be fine. I love you."

'Buela pats my back and runs off to call her friend from the doctor's office, Mr. Jagoda, to make sure he knows the exact time he needs to pick me up for the Philadelphia airport. I'm not sure what I'll talk to him about, but a free ride was too good to resist. Malachi's aunt will be taking him, and although some of the other kids were coordinating rides, Pretty Leslie is the only other person who lives near me, and she didn't ask for a ride and I for damn sure didn't offer. I pick Babygirl out of her crib — I really need to get on buying her a bed — and she snuggles in next to me.

This time tomorrow I'll be in Spain. And this is the most excited and scared I've been since I birthed this little being. For a whole week I'll be able to birth a new version of myself. And I can't wait.

Arrival

The moment the wheels land on the tarmac, I let go of the breath I didn't know I'd been holding. It's afternoon here, six hours ahead of Philly, and from the airplane windows as we landed I got a view of the city of Madrid: big city blocks and red-roofed houses.

Next to me, Amanda squeezes my hand. Richard squeezes hers. Throughout the flight the whole class kept getting up and talking to one another, walking down the aisles in our socks, and probably being way too Philly for a flight to Europe, but none of us cared. I was able to sit next to Malachi and nap on his shoulder throughout the flight, but the flight attendant had people return to their assigned seats for the landing.

We are giddy as a bunch of little kids in a brand-new playground. Some of us, like me, are on a plane for the first time in our lives. The airplane food wasn't as bad as people make it out to seem. And the flight attendants were super sweet. They even giggled when Malachi jokingly asked for a white wine with his dinner, although at Chef Ayden's loud "Young man," from a couple of rows back, they quickly wiped the smiles off their faces, although their eyes still twinkled.

Getting our suitcases is a hot mess because some people (Pretty Leslie) thought it was a good idea to bring two suitcases and a duffel bag, although we're only here a week. We have to wait for the luggage and then we move through customs. Chef walks around counting us over and over again as if one of us might have decided this was a bad idea and climbed back onto the plane. Malachi leans against the wall with me as we wait for everyone else, and kicks my foot gently.

"We're here," he says, and then smiles.

"We're *almost* here," I say back, and I know my smile matches his. We still have a bus to take to Sevilla. But still, we are in Spain. Somehow, we made it happen. I look around at all of us, a colorful group of Americans. Not just our skin, although we are colorful in that sense too, but just everything about us. The fitteds, the Jordans and Foams, the cutoff jeans, the bright lipstick and fresh sweats would make you think we were getting off a video shoot and not an eight-hour flight. We look beautiful and hood and excited to see the world, and none of us are hiding from this world seeing us. All of us shining despite what it took us to earn our way here.

ROOMMATES

The bus that picks us up for the five-hour trip to Sevilla is small and we have to sit hip to hip. Chef hurls his bulky body into the front seat and begins talking in rapid Spanish to the driver — I didn't even know he spoke Spanish.

"What's he saying?" Malachi whispers in my ear. His breath tickles my neck and it feels so good I almost let out a little sigh before I catch myself. Don't get caught up, Emoni. *That* is not what you're here for. I scoot over, trying not to make it seem like I'm scooting over.

"That they're taking us hostage to an underground black market," I say with a straight face. "Something about Liam Neeson coming to save us."

He flings his arm around my shoulder. "You're a cornball, Santi."

The bus starts moving and I press my face against the window. I take in the large churches, the tall buildings that look like elegant wedding cakes, the city center and monuments. As we leave the city behind us, I watch the landscape as Malachi naps with his head on my shoulder. I see so many green fields and squat trees with purple flowers and I find them all beautiful, but then I doze off, too.

A cheer from the front of the bus wakes me up. We are finally in Sevilla, if the welcome sign on the road in front of us is to be believed. The streets are paved in cobblestones, and all the little shops have wide awnings that give off shade. We circle through a plaza where men and women sit cuddled up on benches and eating ice cream. It doesn't look very different from the States except there are a lot of tan white folks and more colorful architecture; the bricks on the houses, bright pinks and yellows; and trees with bright fruit that shines even in the dark. We pass a family sitting on the corner, holding a sign. They are olive-skinned, with dark hair and colorful skirts.

"Oh, look," Leslie says, pointing. "Gypsies. I read they have a lot of them here." The smallest one is a child about Emma's age, wearing a red vest and short pants. He bangs the cup he's using to collect money on the cobblestones. The van starts moving again and we pass crowds standing outside bars, then cross a bridge into what seems like a more residential area.

"I read that word isn't what they liked to be called," Malachi says to me, but he says it loud enough for everyone, including Pretty Leslie, to hear him.

The van pulls up into the parking lot of a bakery where a group of people are waiting for us. They're older, with thick waists, mostly women.

Chef shifts in the front seat so he can look at us. All ten of his sleepy teen chefs. "Okay, group. These people will be the host families you will stay with this week. In the morning we'll meet back here for different tours, you will return to your host family for lunch and siesta, and in the afternoon you will each serve as a chef's apprentice for one of the eateries in the area. Any questions?"

I look around then raise my hand. "Are we staying alone?"

"Why, you want Malachi to go with you?" Pretty Leslie says, and some of the other girls laugh. I'm glad it's dark so no one can see my blushing face.

"Emoni, that's a great question. You will be staying in pairs. And actually, Leslie, you're roommates with Emoni."

THE FIRST NIGHT

Señorita Mariana is younger than 'Buela, but I don't think it's by much, and unlike the other housemothers, she is slim and trim. She immediately grabs my book bag and is reaching for one of Pretty Leslie's rollies, but Pretty Leslie swerves away.

"No, it's okay. I got it." She pulls all her bags protectively to her.

I smile at Señorita Mariana. "You don't have to carry my bag," I say in English. I hope she understands because I am not looking forward to breaking out my Spanish! I only speak that with 'Buela.

Señorita Mariana cocks her head to the side. "Está bien. I can help. You just got off a bus." She holds my bag and begins walking. I look over at Pretty Leslie, who shrugs. We both follow. It's a winding hill downward, and I struggle to keep my bag from rolling away from me. When Mariana turns into a storefront and opens the door I see that it's an old-school music store.

She turns on the light and motions for us to follow her. "The apartment is upstairs. My kids marry and leave. Follow me." She hustles up the stairs in her long purple skirt, still carrying my suitcase. Pretty Leslie follows behind us, all red and out of breath, hauling up her bags as best she can.

"Girl, stop trying to prove something," I say, and grab a bag from her. She must be really winded because she doesn't even protest.

The upstairs is nice and airy with a small kitchen and living room. Mariana points to the back.

"Bathroom that way. Bedroom this way." She walks through a small hallway and turns on the light to a room on the left. Inside are two twin beds, a dresser, and a large wooden crucifix over the mirror. "I will let you get settled. If you need something, I will be in the kitchen warming up dinner. You come ask." She smiles and pushes her hair away from her face, looking expectant as if we might already have questions for her. I smile back and shrug. Pretty Leslie shakes her head. When Mariana leaves she pounces on the bed farthest from the doorway.

"If that lady is crazy and tries to kill us in the middle of the night I'm not going to be the one to die first."

I roll my eyes. "We're in another country and you're acting like a brat," I say, and take out my clothes, folding them into smaller squares to fit into the dresser's drawers.

"Whatever. I'm not acting like anything. You just love being liked so much with your smiley-smiley self."

She pulls out a pair of sweats from her smaller suitcase, pushes the two suitcases into a corner and her third bag under her bed, and leaves the room.

Ms. Mariana, Pretty Leslie, and I eat a dinner of oily rice and steak in absolute silence, the dwindling daylight finally giving all of us an excuse to go to bed early.

■ ■ ■ ■

In our room, I notice that the air here smells different. Like oranges. I turn on the small night lamp, quickly throw on sweats and a T-shirt, and pull off my bra through my sleeve. I crawl into bed.

Although I would never let Babygirl skip brushing her teeth, I want to be asleep too badly to worry about my oral hygiene tonight. I can brush my teeth in the morning. When Pretty Leslie comes into the room, I turn the light off and stare at the ceiling. I wonder what 'Buela and Emma are up to. It's still afternoon there. My eyes adjust to the darkness and I look at Pretty Leslie's dark form huddled in her bed.

"Do you think you'll get homesick?" I ask.

"Girl, don't try to talk to me like we're cool," she says through her teeth, and rolls over on the bed so her back is to me.

"I know it's only a week but I haven't ever been away from home this long. It all looks so different than Philly."

I can imagine her rolling her eyes at me. "Like you told me earlier, it's only seven days. You'll be okay. Plus, isn't one of your parents some kind of Spanish? Haven't you ever been to the Dominican or whatever?"

"I'm half Puerto Rican. And no, I've never been anywhere outside of Philly."

Pretty Leslie's only response is a loud snore.

CHEF AMADI

"Buenos días, clase, mi nombre es Elena Amadí, and I make modern Spanish cuisine with a North African twist." The woman at the front of the room is young-ish, maybe only ten years older than us. She has long dark hair and even in her chef's outfit you can tell she works out. Angelica would call her a hottie and I'd have to agree. We are all in a large kitchen, and Chef Amadí is the last of seven chefs to introduce herself. The whirring fan hanging from the ceiling has done little to stop us from getting sweaty, and although we were excited this morning when we took a tour of the ancient military watchtower, most of us are looking like we're about to fall dead asleep on our feet.

"I'm not going to make it, Santi," Malachi whispers. "Catch me if I faint."

I roll my eyes at him. "You just gon' fall then, with your big self."

Chef Ayden clears his throat with that rumble of his. "Okay. Now that everyone has met the chefs, I will tell you who you will be apprenticing with this week. I took into account your strengths and inclinations and paired you with someone you can not only be a help to, but also learn from.

"Amanda, you'll be at the bakery down the block with Chef Juan. Richard, you'll be making tapas across the street with Chef Joselina. Malachi, butchery for you with Enrique, learning to make cured meat." He's at the very bottom of the list when he looks up. "Emoni, you'll be working with Chef Amadí. Modern cuisine with a twist — sounds just like you."

CLUCK, CLUCK

"Emoni, I'm looking forward to working
with you this week. First, let me learn
what you already know. Can you name
me these ingredients?" Chef Amadí
points to the different herbs and spices.
"I can see that you know," she says. And
I *do* know.

I pick up the large leaf and sniff it. It's
smaller than the type we use back home
but I'd know that scent anywhere. "That
one's bay leaf," I say. "And that seed is
cardamom."

She nods and shoots me a wink.

She moves us to a different station and
opens a container where several large
octopi chill on beds of ice. I've never
worked with octopus and I'm fascinated
by the vibrant red color of the skin and
the slippery feeling of it in my hands. She

demonstrates with a knife how to slice through the octopus tentacles that she will marinate for grilling. I pull my hands back when they begin reaching for the spices. I feel like scolding them as if they were Babygirl, always trying to touch something they have no business touching. Babygirl. I was able to FaceTime 'Buela and Babygirl right before I got here and it felt so good to see their faces.

"Chef Amadí," I say, comfortable enough to ask something I've been wondering about. "One of the kids from school has your same last name, but with an 'h.' Ahmadi. I didn't realize it was Spanish."

"My family hails from Morocco," Chef Amadí says. Her voice always sounds like it's in song. I look at her. Her skin has a tinge of tan in it, but I wouldn't have thought her anything other than a Spaniard. I slow my knife down and glance at her under my lashes.

"Oh, no. You probably can't see it. I take after my father's side, mostly Spanish. But Spain and all of the Iberian Peninsula has a huge influence of the Moors."

I didn't know a lot of this. I don't know how to respond so I grab another tentacle and sprinkle it with oil.

"Chef Ayden says you have something special. An 'affinity with the things that come from the dirt,' he says. A master of spices. And coming from Ayden that means a lot. He doesn't usually believe in natural inclinations. Only in working hard enough to make the hard work seem effortless. Is it true about you?"

I know my eyebrows look about ready to parachute off my face. "You mean the bay-leaf thing?"

"No more oil, that's good." She takes the bowl of marinated octopus from my hand, covers it with a red cloth, and puts it in the fridge. "The 'bay-leaf thing' is exactly what I mean. You're new to Spain. From what your teacher tells me, not many of you have had exposure to world cuisines. Yet, you know a variety of herb that looks and smells slightly different when found outside of this region. I'm sure you've probably seen it in other ways. You've probably mixed spices together no one told you would go together. Cut a vegetable in a certain way that you believe will render it more flavorful. You *know* things that no one has taught you, sí?"

I shake my head no at her. 'Buela always said I had magic hands but I've never said it out loud about myself. And I don't know if I believed it was magic as much as I believed I'm a really good cook. But she is right; most of my experimenting is with spices. "My aunt Sarah sends me recipes that I practice with. And I watch a lot on Food Network. Do you have that channel here? It's really good. They have this show called *Chopped* —"

Chef Amadí puts down the rag she was wiping down the counter with and takes my hands in hers. Studies my palms. "Chef Ayden tells me you have a gift. If you don't want to call it magic, fine. You have a gift and it's probably changed the lives of people around you. When you cook, you are giving people a gift. Remember that."

I pull my hands from hers. "What's next?" I ask.

Chef Amadí purses her lips, then takes a breath and smiles. "You're going to make hen for my guests. The restaurant opens for lunch in an hour and a half. We will call it the Monday special."

Her words scurry over my heart like a barrio rat and I want to squeal out a horrified "Me?" But I keep my face calm and nod like I cook for dozens and dozens of people every day with a recipe I haven't tried before.

She nods. "Take whatever spices you want, break down the bird in any form. We will serve it your way. Gallina à la Americana."

She raises an eyebrow and I know it's a challenge. She's trying to see if I can hang. I adjust my chef's hat and walk to the pantry. I don't have to turn around to know that Chef Amadí is smiling.

"Gallina à la Afro-Boricua has a better ring to it."

GAME TIME

Chef Amadí's restaurant isn't big. Only five or six tables, and she says usually only twenty to thirty patrons show up on a regular afternoon. She's hired two local college students as her serving staff and cleanup crew. Both girls smile and wave at me but seem as shy to whip out their English as I am to try my Spanish.

I don't think about talking to them for too long because I've got hen to prepare. I think about what Chef Ayden taught us in regard to the ratios needed, and although it takes me a bit, I calculate that we'll need eight to ten pounds of hen. I've never had to prep that much meat at one time. I come up with a quick spice mix and make sure to keep as close to my recipe as possible so that the results are similar across the board.

When the bell rings over the entryway I wipe the back of my wrist across my sweat-speckled forehead. An hour and some change has passed in the blink of an eye. Chef Amadí winks at me and goes to greet the customers. It's game time. The next four hours move at light speed, and when I look up to check the time, I'm covered in sweat and we are completely out of the special. We moved from lunch to early dinner about an hour ago but my shift with Chef Amadí spans noon to five p.m. She told me she'll close for an hour and regroup, then open back up for dinner. I unbutton my jacket and take off my hat before stepping out into the dining room.

"Chef Amadí, the hen was just so good! There was something spicy, peppercorn or chili?" a patron asks. He is a big man with a protruding belly and multiple chins; his eyes sparkle and his cheeks are red, probably from the table wine. I like him as soon as he begins to compliment the special.

"Thank you, Don Alberto. It's my sous chef's recipe," she says, and gestures toward me.

"Señorita, delicioso. ¿Qué te puedo decir? ¡Me lambí los dedos!" he says, and I smile but other than a mumbled "Gracias, señor," I don't say anything else. I also hope he didn't really lick his fingers since he's shaking my hand pretty hard and I'd rather not have his saliva all over me despite how much I like him.

Don Alberto furrows his eyebrows, still holding my hand in his. He begins murmuring, still in Spanish. "Can I tell you the oddest thing about your hen? I've been having a bad day. Everything was going wrong, including my stove not wanting to turn on, which is why I came out for dinner, on a Monday of all days! But from the first bite of your food . . . it reminded me of my favorite aunt. Sitting at her knee when she told me stories and shucked peas." His voice gets rough at the end and I give his hand a small squeeze.

Chef Amadí smiles at him. "I'll bring your table another bottle of wine. I'm glad you enjoyed the special."

I look around. Several tables have at least one person who ordered the hen. I see the bones and smile. The plates look licked clean.

"You did well, Emoni." Chef Amadí looks at her watch. "Oh! But you need to go. You will miss your own supper with your group. We'll clean up here, don't worry."

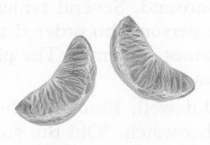

WINNING

When I get to the rooftop paella restaurant where our group has a table, I see that everyone looks how I feel. Like a bulb has been turned on beneath our skin.

Everyone at the table is too excited to shut up. We play with our dinner forks and recount our days. What our chefs or sponsors asked us to do, what we cut and measured. Pretty Leslie is shadowing a line cook. Richard is working at a seafood market and Amanda is at a bakery. When Malachi asks what station I was working at, I shrug.

"You saw how small a place it was. No stations, really. Chef Amadí had me prepare the daily special."

Even though Pretty Leslie is three seats

away from me she must be ear-hustling hard because she leans in halfway across the table to ask, "The whole meal? On your first day?"

I shrug again and don't answer. In the moment I didn't even consider how much I was being challenged. I just put my head down and got to work. But I guess not all of us were being challenged in that same way.

Chef Ayden looks calmer and happier than he did in our classroom. "I'm glad you all are learning so many different things."

I look down at my cold soup, a gazpacho, and try not to smile. Then I sneak off to the bathroom so I can use the restaurant Wi-Fi to FaceTime with 'Buela. Babygirl is at her daycare, but at least I can hear 'Buela's voice and get an update on things back home.

THE ROOTS

"Good girl," Chef Amadí says as she peers over my shoulder. I clip the parsley leaves. "Now smell them, what next?"

I look at the other dirt beds in the backyard garden. Chef Amadí doesn't have any of them labeled — she says their names don't matter, only where they tell her they want to be.

"Are you listening to them?" I nod even though I'm not listening. I don't even know what that means. I'm pretty sure the basil and parsley aren't talking to me. It's that something tugs at my hands telling me what needs to go where next. I walk a loop around the garden and snip a bit here, a bit there. When I finish my circle, Chef looks at the bundle I hold out to her.

"Muy bien. Today we have rabbit and mushrooms on the menu. What should we pair it with?" she asks, but she's already stepping into the restaurant, opening the big refrigerator door. She looks at me.

"Rabbit with harissa," I say, closing my eyes. "Rice with mushrooms, rich with saffron."

Later, in our bedroom I tell Pretty Leslie about my day. Less because I think she cares and more because my FaceTime with 'Buela was really me cooing at Babygirl. Seeing her eclipsed any excitement I might feel about my day. Although it's only been three days, I already miss hearing her small feet pattering all over the house, her high-pitched voice singing along to *Moana*.

But I still need to tell someone about my strange afternoon. There was no time at dinner to talk to Malachi.

"She has you doing what?" Leslie says as she parts her hair so she can Bantu knot it. I look at the lines between her knots and notice some of them aren't straight. I wouldn't let Babygirl walk out the house with such uneven parts.

"She sounds like a crackhead. I always knew that lady was crazy, got you sniffing herbs and shit." The offer I was going to make to part her hair dies in my mouth.

"Don't you think 'crackhead' is a strong word? You don't even know her."

Pretty Leslie still rolls her eyes and sucks her teeth every time she speaks to me, but I'm starting to think it has less to do with my friendship with Malachi and more that it's just the way she speaks to people.

"Fine. She sounds crazy. Shouldn't she be teaching you the basics? Chop and dice and mince. Devein shrimp. That's what the rest of us are doing, not sniffing herbs." She shrugs. "Definitely not talking to food."

I massage my feet. Chef advised all of us to buy a pair of thick-soled clogs since we'd be spending most days on our feet, and now I wish I had listened, because my Air Maxes are not comfortable for all the hours I'm on my feet.

"Do you wanna be a chef, Leslie?" I

384

ask without looking up. I can only imagine her screw-face. I wait for her sarcastic response but it never comes. When I finally do look at her she's rolling a puff of hair into a twist and knotting it into a neat little stack.

"Leslie?"

She shrugs. "I don't know, girl. Everyone wants to know what I'm going to be. I'm the first person to graduate high school in my family. First person to ever get a passport. I been lucky to make it this far without dropping out or having a kid. No offense. My life at home . . . it isn't the easiest. I just want to see how far I can get. But I don't know if I'm made to be a chef — I can't talk to plants and shit." She smirks. "I just know whatever it is, I want it to be major. I want to be remembered for something great. I want to leave a skyscraper-sized mark on the world that reminds people: Leslie Peterson was fucking here."

I look at Pretty Leslie and remember what Malachi once told me about her being more than she seemed. Maybe he was right, because I know just what she means.

To: SarahFowlkes_15@exchange.com
Date: Tuesday, March 31, 11:48 PM
Subject: hi!

Hey Aunt Sarah,

I just want you to know, your cobbler recipe is making the rounds here in Andalusia. That's the name for the southern region of Spain where Sevilla is located. So, your cobbler traveled from the South of the US to the south of the Iberian Peninsula! I let the peaches sit in the juice of some sour oranges and added apricots, and the patrons at the restaurant I'm working at gobbled it up before the lunch rush was over!

Thanks for asking about Babygirl. 'Buela says she's been fussing and throwing tantrums and it's probably the change in not having me around. She's fine when I talk to her on the phone, but it's not really easy for either one of us. She's going to stay with her father's family starting tomorrow, so hopefully that will help her fall into a familiar routine at his house.

There are so many things I've tried here that I wish I could fold into an email and send your way. I've had amazing gelato, and coffee. Some incredible cheese and fried squid and sausage made from suckling pig (I know you don't eat pork, but trust me, it was smack-your-momma good). I probably won't be trying to re-create any of that anytime soon, but I had these little cookies pow-dered with sugar and when I try it at home I'll send you my version of the recipe.

Attached is a picture the chef I'm ap-prenticing for took today. Don't I look all focused and professional, or what-ever? That salad is getting some Emoni-inspired work! Thinking of you.

Sending you lots of love & a bit of
cinnamon dust,
E

CHECK-IN

It's our fourth day in Spain, and half the class is buzzing. It's officially April 1 and a lot of college acceptances will be rolling in, in the morning East Coast time. Some people keep wasting their data checking their phones for updates.

I've already made up my mind that I won't check mine until I get back home. Amanda is going into a job-training program straight from graduation so although she smiles at our excited classmates, she also doesn't seem as pressed as everyone else. Pretty Leslie looks bored as usual, like the only care she has in the world is the chip in her manicure.

Instead of starting with our usual morning tour guide, Chef Ayden has an announcement.

"All right, class. Your instructors tell me that with the exception of one or two of you" — Chef points a finger at Malachi — "most of you are doing really well."

We all laugh and I elbow Malachi in the ribs. He smirks and bends down so his mouth is super close to my ear. "They just don't want the rest of you to feel bad. I'm actually the best student here. My cuts of jamón ibérico would make you believe in God."

I bite back a chuckle at his exaggerated Spanish pronunciation.

"Ahem." Chef coughs into his hand and raises an eyebrow at me. "Instead of a moderated tour this morning, I thought you all could have some free time today and explore the city. Just don't go farther than the old city walls. And don't forget your shifts begin at noon."

He shoos us out. "Emoni, a moment?"

I wait for everyone to walk away, but I see Malachi standing near the bottom of the hill, clearly waiting for me.

"I just wanted to make sure you were okay with Chef Amadí? We went to culinary school in Paris together and I know she can be a bit intense."

Whoa. I didn't know that's how they knew each other. "At Le Cordon Bleu?" I don't know much about culinary institutes but even I know that's one of the most famous and best schools for cooking in the world.

He nods and I realize then I don't know much about Chef Ayden or how he came to be our instructor, but I'm glad he is. And I'm glad to be paired with Chef Amadí. "Chef Amadí has been great. I couldn't imagine working with anyone else."

"Great. I'm happy it's working out. Get going; I don't want to cut too much into your free morning." And then as I walk down the hill I hear him yell out, "And don't spend too much time with Malachi. He's a bad influence, that kid!" But he has laughter in his voice when he says it and I can tell he made sure he was loud enough for Malachi to hear him.

Malachi is laughing when I reach him. He scoops my hand in his and we walk in silence behind the rest of the group, and for a single moment I feel like the sunlight sneaking over the hill is also sneaking inside me.

GILDED

When I was little the other kids from the block and I would get together and play a game called mancala. It's a fast-paced board game where the pieces are these glass stones that are round on one side and flat on the other. Each stone is a beautiful color: red, blue, teal, clear shot through with squiggles of gold. I used to cradle those stones in my hand, more interested in holding them up to the light than playing the game. Even then I knew they weren't real gems, but when I held them in my hand I felt like a rich queen, like I was holding something precious.

That's how I feel about the Catedral de

Sevilla. Like I want to cradle the whole thing in the palm of my hand and hold it up to the light and watch it glint and glimmer. There are all these portraits of famous popes and leaders, and everything from the floor to the ceiling is made of gold and silver. I stop turning in a wide circle and my eyes land on sculptures in a corner of the cathedral. In the center is a coffin being held up by four figures — each one dressed in dark metal and gold armor and crowns; the two in the front have a staff in their outside hands and the two in the back have the hand not holding the casket on their hip.

I go stand next to a tour group so I can listen in on what their guide is saying. "And this is the tomb of Christopher Columbus." I move even closer as the guide describes the remains in the tomb and how different parts of the world claim different pieces of Columbus's body for the honor of being able to say they have his final resting place.

Malachi circles over. "You good, Santi?"

I nod. But I don't know if I am. I walk away from the group to the other side of the massive casket and Malachi follows.

"Do you know what the word 'Boricua' means?"

Malachi shakes his head. "I know it's what all my Puerto Rican homies call themselves."

"I've already told you my father is a big history buff when it comes to PR, and he doesn't need much prompting to remind me that before Columbus, Puerto Rico was called 'Borinken' by the Taíno people who lived there. He told me once it means 'Land of the brave and noble lords.' If he were here now he would be so pissed. All over the world there are monuments to Columbus, museums trying to claim a piece of his body as if he were a saint. And look at this here, all this gold they use to honor him, gold they got from our island in the first place, and hardly anyone remembers the enslaved people who dug through the rivers for that gold, who were there before he arrived. Whose descendants are still there now."

And suddenly, the cathedral isn't so pretty to me anymore despite all its gold and glitter.

HISTORIES

We walk outside the cathedral and I'm still quiet. Julio is always lecturing me about who we are, but I usually only listen with one ear. I definitely don't get as hyped as he does. Until today. Seeing that statue of Columbus really hit home. Sometimes it seems like being Puerto Rican is such a fact of life that I forget not everyone hand-washes their panties, or eats pernil at Thanksgiving, or has some traditions and names for things that are African and Taíno: mofongo, cassava. People don't realize that Spain is a complicated place for someone like me. I just can't shake off how much it feels that this place, Spain, and this city, Sevilla, are tied to who I am even if I'm not sure I want to be tethered to them.

"Want to see the castle, Santi?" Malachi

brushes my arm. I don't know how he knows I'm in a weird funk but he does. I nod. We enter the Alcázar, and I'm surprised; the castle looks nothing like I expected. It's as beautiful as the rest of old Sevilla, but seems to belong to a different country: high arches, six-pronged stars carved into the stone walkway, orange trees blooming along the perimeter.

"What is different about this part of the palace?" a tour guide asks her group in English. We join in when we see Pretty Leslie and Amanda are a part of it. "Does anyone know?"

We all shake our heads, and I'm surprised when Malachi raises his hand.

"It's paying homage to Islam." He points to the ceiling. "The star and moon. And that bell over there looks like a call to prayer."

"Exactly right! This is one of the few palaces that shows the Muslim conquest of Spain in 711 AD."

I look around. This is a place where two worlds collided. Beautiful because of the struggle that happened to create it. Holy because of the belief people had in it. A home, a masterpiece of art, a mixture of different cultures.

"How did you know that?" I whisper to Malachi. Something about this place makes me feel a need to whisper.

"I'm from Newark." He shrugs. "And you from Philly, so you should know every other Black kid is probably Muslim. Plus, Malcolm X is my hero. And when I was younger and read his autobiography, I began to study Islam. Still figuring it out, but I picked up a lot when I visited the mosques. And although I'm a beast in science, history is my favorite class."

How didn't I know he studied Islam? How didn't I know about his love of history? "There's so much about you I still don't know." And suddenly I want to know everything. I want to ask him all of the things. I want to kiss the deep dimple in his cheek. Maybe it's because we are not at home anymore, but I feel free: free to say what I want, to feel what I feel, without having to think of every single action and reaction.

"Hey, how about ice cream later?" I ask. "After dinner?"

His smile grows bigger and he raises a

brow. "You asking me on a date, Santi? You know ice cream is the way to my heart."

I bite my lip. I don't know if I want his whole heart yet, but I also don't know if I would mind having it. We've entered a rose garden. A twisty maze that has big orange trees hanging over the bushes. A plaque near the entrance says that a Muslim emperor built it for his wife. "Yeah, Malachi, I think I am."

"Shhh." Pretty Leslie hushes us from the front of the group. "Some of us are trying to learn! Y'all so damn rude."

And I wonder how many other Black Puerto Rican Philly teens have laughed in this orange-tree garden built for a queen.

THE CHASE

After dinner that night, when we get to the meeting point where we go our separate ways, Chef gives us a little wave. "Make sure you all get to your host family house safely. Remember, you're guests, so get there as soon as possible."

Pretty Leslie and I might be the only two people who actually *have* been going home on time. I've been hearing stories in the morning of people going out dancing and to bars. They keep talking about trying absinthe, which is impossible to find in stores in its strongest form in the States, so folks are way too hype to try it.

"Emoni, you coming home?" Pretty

Leslie yells from halfway up the hill to our homestay. I shake my head. And she looks from me to Malachi through narrowed eyes.

"Pretty Leslie didn't handle the end of y'all talking well, did she?" I ask Malachi as we take a turn that leads not to the house but to another little street. The streets of Sevilla have ice-cream shops sprinkled on almost every block the way Papi stores and Starbucks are back home. I pass an ice-cream shop every morning and I know it's exactly the kind of place Malachi would love. I lead the way.

He shrugs. "She and I had an honest conversation. I told you from the beginning I thought she was a cool girl, and I still think so . . . even if she says some dumb shit when she's trying to pretend she doesn't care what people think."

I want to ask for more details, but I figure it's not my business. Although Malachi says he was only her friend, I wonder if she wanted to be more.

Malachi takes my hand. His long fingers close over my own and he tugs me to him when we pass a couple on the street. I look over at him. His dark brown cheeks, his high forehead. The wisps of hair on his chin and the sideburns shaped into a perfect Philly point. He's not smiling, and I want to make him smile more than anything. He's a different person when he smiles, a friendlier Malachi that I imagine is someone I can talk to about this Malachi standing next to me that I don't know what the hell to do with.

The streetlights glint against the stone streets. My hand is still in Malachi's and he gives it a light squeeze before sticking his hands in the pockets of his black jacket and pulling my hand in with him. Outside of a restaurant a man plays a guitar and sings a slow, sad song that sounds like it comes from the bottom of his gut.

This moment is one I don't ever want to end. And my breath stops short. This is exactly why I don't hang out with guys. Angelica would tell me I'm being stupid, since I don't hang out with girls, either. And she would be right. This is why I don't get close to people. Because it makes it too easy to hurt them. Be hurt by them.

I stop walking and Malachi stutters to

a halt. I pull up on my tippy-toes, grip the hand that's holding mine, and begin meeting his mouth for a kiss, when I feel a sharp tug on my shoulder and I drop my hands to see that a little kid has taken off, clutching my purse.

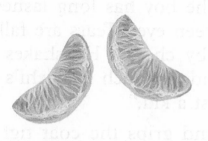

CHILDREN

Malachi is right behind him before I can even get a breath out. The little boy is quick and ducks around people and pivots hard into different alleyways. I follow as close as I can, keeping sight of Malachi. He never loses a beat. For a split second between gasping for air it hits me what it must have been like for him growing up in Newark if his eyes are so sharp and his reflexes so fast that he can keep up with a young boy in a city he doesn't know. I also realize that I need to start working out with Angelica, because I fall far behind after the second block. Then Malachi has the boy by the back of his coat and I speed up before he can hurt him.

"Hey, it's okay," I say, taking back the

purse. The boy has long lashes framing bright green eyes. Tears are falling down his grubby cheeks. He shakes in Malachi's hands. I touch Malachi's shoulder. "He's just a kid."

His hand grips the coat tighter. "Ask him why."

I touch his hand. "Mal, stop. He wanted money. Let him go."

"Ask him why, Emoni." He never uses my first name. I clutch my purse tight in one arm and turn to the child.

"¿Porqué robaste la cartera?" I ask him. My words come out slow as I try to remember each one and make sure I'm saying them right. I've always understood Spanish better than I've spoken it, but I must have gotten my question across since the boy's eyes widen even more when he looks at me.

His own Spanish sounds garbled because he's talking through tears. "I wouldn't have if I knew you two were black," he says, and I almost laugh. "I didn't see you from the front."

"Not being black would have made a difference?"

He runs a hand across his runny nose, avoids Malachi's hands. "Everyone knows you guys run fast."

"Not all of us. Just like not all of you steal, right?"

He looks down at the ground. "My baby sister, she's hungry. My parents don't like it, but we beg. Because we're cuter." He blinks innocently and smiles sadly. And he's right — I would have given him money. He's cute as hell.

I look up at Malachi. He still hasn't let go of the boy, but his eyes seem far away. He snaps his attention back to me when I speak. "He was hungry. He says he has a sister who's hungry, too."

"Tell Little Man to take us to her. I want to see where they are staying."

"Malachi, let go of him. You're scaring him and we can't force him to take us to his family if he doesn't want to. I have my purse back. It's not that serious."

But the boy must understand some English because he points into an alleyway not too far from us. A small face is peeking out around the wall. Malachi drops his hand from the boy's shoulder.

Malachi doesn't say anything. I reach into my bag and pull out five euros. I put them in the little boy's palm and he runs to the little girl, scooping her up and walking deep into the alleyway and out of sight.

"I just can't get over how young they are," I say to Malachi. She was only two or three years older than Babygirl. I turn to Malachi, but he's still watching the darkness that the two kids ran into.

I pat his arm. "You okay? Out of breath? That was quite a sprint." I'm hoping I can joke him out of his silence, but he just blinks in the direction of the kids and then shakes his head.

"My mother always told me one of the hardest things to be in a hungry world is a parent. But sometimes I think it's being an older brother. To know exactly what your sibling needs and not have the age or strength to know any way to get it for them." He smirks but his smile is empty.

I put my hand in his and squeeze. "Let's go get ice cream."

"No, I don't want ice cream anymore, Santi."

He pulls on one of my curls and I don't know if it's the sadness in his smile or his faraway look, but next thing I know, I'm arching up and holding his face between my hands. I place my thumb where his dimple would be if he were smiling. His hands move to my waist and I can feel their warmth through my jacket. He doesn't pull me closer or push away but I understand he needs to feel close, and I need that, too.

SMOOCH

His lips are soft. I'd forgotten how soft lips can be. It's been a long time since I kissed someone. His hands tighten in my jacket but other than that he's still. I step in closer, angle my head, move my hands to the back of his neck, and pull his face closer. He opens his mouth, and I bite on his bottom lip, then I'm not thinking, I'm not planning the next step. His hand moves down to my butt and curves around it.

A wolf whistle breaks through the sound of my heartbeat and heavy breathing. "¡Pero mira eso!" A drunk couple hoots and hollers at us.

"C'mon." Malachi grabs my hand and we walk back to the street we came from.

He stops and pulls me toward him. Then he's kissing me again. And I can't think because his hands move up and down my coat and the back of my jeans, and he smells so good. And I can't remember Tyrone ever touching me like this, like this body was a dream he was afraid to wake up from.

"Santi, you blushing? I make you shy or something?" he says, and hugs me to him. "Santi, what am I supposed to do with you?"

I snuggle into his sweater. "Nothing. We should just enjoy it. We're in goddamn Europe, across the world; no one needs us right now. We should just . . ." I shrug. "Be."

"And when we get back?"

I think about Babygirl. How I wake up every day expecting to see her crib and how it clogs my throat with tears not to be near her. How I miss 'Buela's shuffling slippers, and her yelling directions at the Eagles' quarterback. How I need to find a new job and figure out what I'm going to major in if I'm accepted into college. My life when I get back is full of people I love and the responsibilities I

409

have. And I love them, and miss them, but I also want to hold this feeling of freedom tight in my fist, because it has wings and I know as soon as I loosen my grip it will fly straight away. "We figure it out then."

He gives me a long look. "All right, Santi. I'm following you. Where we going next?"

And it seems like he means in terms of directions, but I know he also means in terms of us. Even though it's a Wednesday night, two bars and one club are blaring music from across the street. I point.

Malachi raises an eyebrow and squeezes my hand.

COZY

The bar is small and smoky; when we walk in the bartender is setting a green drink on fire.

A group of Americans take the shots and cheer. Two of them turn around and I see Richard and Amanda. They wave but we don't walk over. Malachi grabs my hand and moves past clusters of people to a small table at the back.

We sit down side by side. I rest my head on his shoulder. "Your sweater is nice."

"You're nicer," he says.

"Yeah? What do you find nice about me?"

Malachi's hand is on my knee and he brushes his fingers up and down my leg.

"Everything. The way you dress, the way you fix your hair. The way you used to tell me we were not friends. It's all nice." I laugh and press my hand against his so it stops moving on my leg.

"I didn't mean to be mean to you before. Well, maybe I did, but I just have a hard time trusting people." I shrug and lift my head from his shoulder. Make a move to scoot away, but he wraps an arm around me and pulls me back.

"What were you saying? Talk to me, Santi," Malachi says, and kisses my ear. It's like now that we've started touching this way and kissing we can't keep our bodies away from each other. But I pull back just enough so that I can look at him.

"When I broke up with Tyrone, when I was pregnant with Babygirl, *after* I was pregnant with Babygirl, guys thought that gave them a reason to be able to come up to me and say anything they wanted, to just grab me or invite me to their houses. They all treated me like a ho." I rub my finger along the tabletop. The wood is sticky with spilled drinks and I put my hand in my lap. "I'm not. I'm not a ho. Not that it should matter if I was, but I'm still not having sex with you."

I know what saying something like that does. Dudes either stop being interested or they think I'm just playing hard to get. But I'm not doing either. I just want to be real clear.

"Look at me, Santi." I keep my eyes firmly on the wooden table. Malachi lowers his face near mine. "I'm serious, look at me."

I look at his ear.

He groans. "At me, Santi, not behind me."

"I was looking at you. At your ear," I mumble, and finally stare into his eyes. I open mine real big so he can tell I see him.

"You're such a smart-ass." He laughs and the fist in my chest curls open its fingers. I take a breath.

"Listen, I don't know what other guys thought. And if you point them out to me when we get back, I'll make sure they never think it again." His voice is dead serious and I believe him. Malachi would fight people for me. I know that already.

"But I'm not those guys. I wanted to talk to you before I knew you had a kid. Wanted to talk to you after you did all your hair flipping, 'we ain't friends,' finger waving —"

"I never waved my finger!"

"— teeth sucking, eye rolling, hip switching, lip pursing, locker-door slamming. All of that was like a damn beautiful dance and I was drawn all the way in. And cool, you don't want to have sex. You've told me you want to take it slow and I get it. But, I been wanting to talk to you since the beginning."

"Just talk?" I raise an eyebrow, and flip my hair, and wave my finger.

Malachi grins and ducks his head. "I mean, you know you fine! At first, I wouldn't have been mad at you if you wanted to do more than talk," he says. "But now, I know my day is better because you are in it and I want to keep you there. I hope I make your day better, too."

UGLY LESLIE

Before I can answer, Richard and Amanda come over, Pretty Leslie trailing like a little ducky behind them. I remember she was on her way home when Malachi and I left for ice cream, but she must have gotten bored by herself. She's loosely holding a drink in her right hand.

"Malachi," Richard says, slightly slurring his words. "Why haven't you got Emoni a drink? You can drink at sixteen here, did you know that? We're celebrating college admissions. I got into Penn!"

"Or rejections," Pretty Leslie says, and takes a big gulp of her drink. Ouch. Maybe Pretty Leslie cared more about admissions than I thought. I try to catch her eyes, see if she's okay, but she won't look at me.

"Oh, Richard! That's wassup! I'm so proud of you." I give Richard's arm a quick squeeze and he instantly ducks his head shyly until a loud burp erupts from his mouth.

"You sure figured out the drinking age quick, huh?" Malachi says, standing up. He stretches and his sweater rises, showing off a bit of skin and muscle. "Congrats on the admission. We should definitely drink to that."

"Yeah, Malachi, get your girlfriend a drink, why don't you?" Pretty Leslie sits down in the seat across from me, and Richard and Amanda fill in the chairs on either side of the table.

"Just some juice?" I say, catching Malachi's eye. The last thing in the world I need is to get in trouble while on a school trip abroad. I remember clearly the waiver we signed, and while I don't mind taking sips of 'Buela's rum or holiday wine, I'll be damned if I get tipsy in another country where I don't know the area or people.

Pretty Leslie shakes her head. "Something with *alcohol,* Emoni. We're in fucking Spain. It's legal here." She takes another big drink from her cup.

I shake my head at Malachi before he walks away. I don't care if it *is* legal. We signed permission slips and I'm not getting in trouble with only two months till graduation.

I lean toward Pretty Leslie. "You feeling all right?"

"I'm fucking dandy, Emoni. How about you? You look like you're having a good ole time."

Pretty Leslie always curses a lot, but usually not with so much bite to her words. The warm fuzzies from the kissing and cuddling with Malachi begin wearing off. I turn to Amanda.

She hands me her cup and whispers in my ear, "Just water; the bakery assignment is different than everyone else's and means I have to be up at, like, four a.m. Have a sip."

I smell it first to make sure. And then take a small drink. It's nice and cold. I smile a thanks at Amanda.

Malachi walks back with two drinks in his hands. One is a dark liquid and has a lime and a cherry. He hands that one to me. From the other one he takes a sip.

I give Amanda back her water and hold the glass Malachi brought me to my lips: Ginger ale, some kind of syrup, a hint of Coke. No liquor, and I know the cherry and lime are just for appearances.

"So what are you two doing here?" Amanda asks, smiling between me and Malachi. She has to know this is awkward because Pretty Leslie definitely likes him, but Amanda can be so oblivious to things, I can't even get angry with her.

"We were just hanging out. We walked around for a bit after dinner and then decided to stop by here," I say.

Pretty Leslie keeps sipping her drink, then downs the whole thing in one gulp. Before I know it, she reaches for my cup and takes a big gulp of that.

"You always gotta be so fucking good." She turns to Richard. "It doesn't even have liquor in it. Look, taste it."

She passes the cup to him and he takes a sip. "Nope. No liquor. I think. I can't

418

even taste things anymore." He puts his head on the wet table and closes his eyes. Amanda rubs his back.

"What's the problem, *Santi*?" Pretty Leslie sings Malachi's nickname for me, and from her lips it sounds distorted. "You don't want to get in trouble with Chef? Don't worry. We won't tell him. We won't tell him you're fucking Malachi, either."

I put my hands on the table to push myself up, but Malachi grabs my arm. "No. We were here first. Leslie, we don't have anything to explain to you. You're mad but you got no reason to be. Don't try to put people's business out there, because we both know you have more than enough business of your own."

"Fuck you, Malachi." Pretty Leslie gets up and tries to walk away, but her fast motions and tipsiness don't seem to mix well because she grabs hold of the table. I stand up, too. She looks like she's about to fall. Then she lowers her head, and bends her body, and throws up all over her shoes. The bar gets quiet at the sound of retching; the bartender points at us.

"Out! Every one of you Americans,

out!" The bartender runs over and he's cursing in Spanish and his accent is so different from what I'm used to that I can't make out every word, but Amanda pulls Richard up, and he takes one look at the vomit and the angry bartender and straightens up his big self quick.

I grab Pretty Leslie and put her arm around my waist, put my arm around her shoulder. She's too drunk or embarrassed to push me away. I give Malachi a little smile. Pretty Leslie is stank, but she's still my roommate.

SETTLED

I let us into Mariana's house quietly and Malachi holds on to Pretty Leslie's other side.

"Are you going to throw up again?" I whisper. No light shines from under Mariana's bedroom door. It's almost one a.m. She usually goes to bed at ten.

"I want my bed." Pretty Leslie's head drops to her chest and then pops back up when she hiccups.

We stagger-walk in the direction of our bedroom and only just manage not to knock over a lamp.

"Hold on a second." I run my hand along the wall and then flip on the switch.

"Ugh. No light," Pretty Leslie says, and plops onto her bed. She curls into a ball. I carefully tug off her vomit-covered

421

sneakers and drop them to the floor, searching the room for somewhere to put them. All I can find is Pretty Leslie's large makeup bag on the chair by her bed. She's going to kill me, but no way I'm sleeping with throw-up shoes hanging out all willy-nilly in the room. I toss the makeup onto the chair and carefully place the shoes into the bag in such a way that I don't actually touch the vomit. I'm going to have to mop the stairs and doorway near the entrance to make sure none of it got into Mariana's house, but Pretty Leslie is going to have to wash her own sneakers. I cover her with the blanket at the foot of her bed.

When I'm done, I stand up straight and blink. Malachi is in the doorway, shaking his head.

I shrug. "I couldn't just leave her like that. I'm a mom."

"You're too good, is what you are." Malachi takes a step forward and I look at him. What does he think we're going to do? Pretty Leslie is drunk but she's alive and she's in the bed right next to mine. And Mariana is on the other side of the apartment.

We both turn and look at the form in the other bed. As if sensing our stares, she turns to the wall and gives a loud burp.

I laugh a little. "I think you'd better leave."

He nods. And we walk to the door. "You could have talked to any of the girls back at Schomburg. Why were you so stuck on me?"

He tugs a curl. "I could only think of you."

I cut my eyes at him. "Malachi," I whisper. "Are you spitting game at me? Is this all so you can get the panties?" I raise an eyebrow but he just shakes his head.

"You ever going to believe me when I say I like you? We only have two more days here," Malachi says. "Think we can spend them together? I'll show you it's more than just that."

He pushes his thumb against my bottom lip. I hadn't even realized I was biting it.

I nod and he gives me a quick kiss.

"Good night."

BOYS WILL BE

The thing is, a part of me is still so afraid to believe Malachi. It had started like this with Tyrone, too. He'd been all smooth with the compliments and the small gifts. Showing up to school to walk me home. Taking me on dates to the movies. I wasn't his first and although he knew he was mine, when his parents insisted he get a paternity test, he didn't defend me.

He also didn't argue when I was five months' pregnant and accused him of cheating. Angelica had friends at his high school and they'd seen him walking around holding hands with some other girl. And when I told him this, said how they'd sent pictures to my phone, he just shrugged. "You're big as a house, what'd you expect me to do?" Just like that. And Tyrone is good with his words. He knows exactly how to make them land soft as a kiss or cut sharp as a pocketknife. So I knew then that he was over us. He wanted to walk away but didn't know how. And I would have respected him if he'd just said, "I don't think this is working for me," instead of saying, "I don't understand why you're getting so mad; you don't even know her." And I could have spit fire the morning he shrugged when I told him he would have to be my baby's father but he could no longer be my man.

And every couple of months he comes back and wants to try to work things out. Or acts jealous if he thinks I'm flirting with someone.

That's what I learned, about him and most guys: who they are when they're giving you flowers and trying to get in your pants is not who they *really* are when it's no longer spring and they've found a new jawn to hang out with. And I know the past isn't a mirror image of the future, but it's a reflection of what can be; and when your first love breaks your heart, the shards of that can still draw blood for a long, long time.

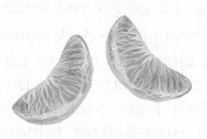

HEART-TO-HEART

Pretty Leslie wakes me mid-dream and for a second, I forget where I am. I think it's Babygirl's voice startling me from sleep until the words penetrate.

"Emoni, I think I drank too much. I feel awful," Pretty Leslie moans from her bed. I flail around trying to find my phone. It's six a.m.

"Good. You should, after drinking so much and talking so greasy to me," I say, sending a quick text to 'Buela saying good morning and asking after Babygirl. She usually goes to sleep by eleven so I know she won't read it for another seven hours, but at least it will be there when she wakes up. I stand. "Lucky you, my grandmother made sure I was a walking pharmacy and I've got some Alka-Seltzer in my bag. I'll go get you some water."

I walk through the dark house, running my hand along the wall to find my way to the kitchen. Pretty Leslie is curled into a ball when I get back to our room. I drop two Alka-Seltzer tablets into the glass and hand it over.

"Here. I think this should help some. My 'Buela swears by this and ginger tea when I have any kind of ache. Does your throat hurt from throwing up so much?"

"I threw up?" Pretty Leslie asks. At least I think that's what she says, since it's muffled by her pillow.

"Yeah, all over your shoes."

She groans and eases her way to sitting in order to take the glass of water from me. She downs the medicine.

"What do you remember?"

"Umm . . ." She bites her lip. "Being at the bar. You and Malachi came in, too, right? I think I sat down with you all, but I don't really remember much else."

I shake my head. "You said some really terrible things. You basically called me a ho. And you embarrassed yourself."

Her eyes widen and for the first time I

see a Leslie who isn't performing the diva, or pouting, or trying to get over on someone. This girl has mascara dust on her cheekbones, her falsies twisted out of shape, and vomit crusted on her lip — a lip that's quivering as if she's about to cry. "Oh my God. How did I get home?"

"Malachi and I brought you back. You drank too much. But I still have something I want to say to you. First, I'm not trying to be better than you and I'm not trying to show you or anyone else up. I've always kept to myself. And I don't know what you and Malachi had going on, but if he didn't want to continue with you, you can't blame me for that. I wasn't out here chasing anybody."

"Oh my God, Emoni. I don't even remember saying those things. I wasn't thinking."

"But it's how you feel, though, right?" I press.

"I mean —" She stops herself midsentence and drinks a big gulp of water. "I really liked Malachi. And I didn't know why he was so into you. But he was — is — and so I —" She shrugs. "I guess I was just angry. Jealous. Everything is

429

always perfect for you. Teachers like you. Your friends are loyal. We get one cute transfer this year and he's in love with you from day one. It just doesn't seem fair."

I shake my head. "Are you kidding? Is that how you see it? Leslie, I have a kid. I've had to go to summer school since I got pregnant to make up for the credits I fell behind on. I had to fight not to be put in a special program for young mothers so I could take senior-level classes and graduate on time with you all. I've worked since I was thirteen and done double that since having a child."

She shrugs again. "I'm not saying it makes sense. It was just hard to like you. I don't really have anyone at home supporting me or pushing me. But even though everyone pitied you at first you just walked through the halls like you were Queen B. Like you couldn't even see us."

I smile. "Well, yeah. How else are you supposed to act when people pity you?"

She smiles back. "Yeah, I guess I hope that if I'd been you I woulda acted the same way. Listen. I was wrong. Malachi ain't the only guy at Schomburg. I'll fall back."

We've shared a lot today, Pretty Leslie and I. And it's the first time I feel like she's being honest with me.

READY?

"Where's your host family?" I ask as I wander through the house. Malachi's host parents are college professors at the local university and are some of the few host parents who speak perfect English.

"They had an event at the school. A reading or something."

I nod and stop in front of one of the paintings in the hall. It's a pretty scene of the city. The light on the stones, the awnings of the marketplace, and the plaza. Malachi tugs on one of my curls before reaching his hand up my neck, to my scalp. It feels good to have him play with my hair.

"What are you thinking about?"

"Nothing. This is a nice painting."

"Are you nervous? To be here with me? I can stop. We can go out or something."

It seems a shame not to enjoy one of our last nights in the city, and a Friday at that, but it *also* seems a shame to waste a perfectly empty apartment. Decisions, decisions.

"Let's just hang out on the couch for a bit before going out. Maybe we can watch TV?"

A Harry Potter marathon is on and I sit with Malachi's arm around me. I translate some of the lines but Malachi has seen the movie before so he can work out a lot of the dialogue without me. We get up to the part when Harry emits his Patronus against a dementor for the first time, when Malachi starts playing with my fingers. Then his hand is on my thigh. I sit still. I want to lean against him.

"You *are* nervous."

I touch a dimple. "Are you a virgin, Malachi?" I've never had the balls to ask, but this seems like something I should know.

He clears his throat and stops playing with my hand. "There was a girl in my last school. We weren't that serious, but we'd fooled around. We'd talked about doing more. But then my brother was shot and I was a mess and my mother told me she was sending me here and then I met you."

I turn my face and he gives me a soft tap kiss and leans back. When I don't move he gives me another tap kiss and it lasts a little longer. The next time he kisses me, I'm on him. Legs straddling his lap, arms wound around his back. Kissing him back.

Tyrone had been fast, and all about him. And it'd been fun the couple of times we did it. Maybe not even fun, as much as it was exciting. It was something new. It was like entering a world everyone talked about but no one knew how to explain, and all of a sudden, you're allowed into the secret. Even if it's not much of a secret. And if I had to count, I'd say we had sex three times at the most. The first time, probably when I got pregnant, and twice after that. I never saw what the big deal was about, outside of how nice it was to be touched. But this is different.

"Are you sure you're a virgin?" I ask him. He kisses like he's been kissing for a long time. And his hands move slowly like they have a precise goal in mind.

"Are you sure you've done this before?" he responds.

I laugh and smack his shoulder. But I *am* nervous. Not because I know tricks or anything — Tyrone and I didn't even do it enough times for me to learn much — but my naked body shows it once carried a child. I dropped the weight quick enough, but it's the other things that show when you aren't wearing clothes that mark you as someone who's given birth. With Tyrone it hadn't even mattered what I knew or didn't know because he knew I didn't know anything. But I feel like Malachi expects things.

"Malachi. I'm not really that experienced. It was only a couple of times. Don't get your hopes —"

He puts a finger up to my lips and keeps kissing my neck. "Please don't bring up other times right now. We can talk later. If you want. But this isn't about other people. We're not here with other people. We're here. Right now. Me and you. Right?"

He keeps kissing my neck. And then my hands are everywhere. I need to touch his skin, his shoulders, his back. I kiss his ear and he moans into my neck.

"That feels too good." And this was new, too. This power of making a boy jump or moan.

I take my shirt off. And he takes off his. "Are you sure?" he asks.

I press a hand to his heart. I'm not sure of anything. "Kiss me again?" So we do, we kiss and we rub, and his hands are on my body and I haven't shown this body to anybody in a long, long time. He rubs a hand along the stretch marks on my breasts and stomach. All the things that mark me as a mom in the most obvious of ways. He kisses me there and everywhere. He reaches for my jeans.

I cover Malachi's hand where it's undoing my zipper and hold it still.

"I think we should wait. It would be romantic. In Spain. Your first time. All of that. It'd be like a story. But . . ."

Malachi puts his hands up and throws his head back on the couch. I start scooting off his lap but he holds me in place. "All good, Santi." He hugs me to himself. "Give me a second to get myself under control."

I brush my fingers on his chest. "Maybe —" I pause. And make myself be brave enough to ask for what I want and not to be rushed into what I'm not ready for. I clear my throat. "Maybe we can try other things?"

He raises an eyebrow, and with more excitement than I've ever seen from him, he gives me a vigorous "Yes, ma'am. Yes, Ms. Santiago. I am your teacher's pet. Blank book. Best student."

I laugh at his straight-up silliness. And this feels right. Whatever we are to become, I'm glad that we can laugh through the uncomfortable moments.

LAST DAY

Even though it's our last full day in Spain and a Saturday, Chef Ayden still has us report to our apprenticeships. I'm working on a marinade for the pork shoulder that Chef Amadí will be serving for dinner tomorrow night. The recipe calls for it to sit in the marinade for a full twenty-four hours, and a part of me wishes I was going to be here one more day so I could try it. But maybe that's the point of a trip like this: you start the process of learning and then you carry it with you back home.

I massage the spice mixture into the pork, pressing firmly.

"Make sure you get a dry rub on the

meat, too. And did you add lemon to that mix?"

"I used sour oranges instead," I say.

"That's good, the sour oranges. Make sure to score the shoulder. Small, shallow cuts to capture all that flavor. I think you've learned here, no?"

I nod and pick up the knife. And I have learned a lot. "Yes, and not just from being in this kitchen." I have learned to cook with confidence, but also to remember the guests have expectations of what I'll serve them. I've learned to trust my hands. But I've learned about more than just food. I've learned about people. From seeing how people from somewhere else walk, and laugh, and love, and eat.

"You have good instincts. You will make a fine chef one day. Maybe when you finish school, you'd like to come back to Spain? I would love to take you on as my apprentice."

I look up quickly and forget what I'm doing. My hand slips and I cut it where I've been holding the pork in place. I drop the knife and quickly back away. "Shit." I check to see if I got any blood on the meat, but Chef Amadí puts her hands on my shoulders and pushes me toward the sink, where she runs water over my hand.

"Oh, here." Chef Amadí wraps a clean towel around my hand. "Keep that water running. Let me see if any got on the food or cutting board. We have Band-Aids and gloves in that cabinet above your head. Only a couple more hours and you would have gone through the trip unscathed. But now you have a war scar to prove you were here."

The small cut stings, but nothing like the tears in my eyes. Being able to stay here, to work in a real kitchen after school and learn more would be a dream. But even as I think it I know I would never want to leave my daughter, or my 'Buela, or the city I love.

"Emoni, it was so wonderful working with you. Anytime you are in Spain you come back here. And if you ever want to talk about working here, I have use for a chef with hands like yours. Oh, and here." Chef Amadí hands me a letter. "This is my official academic evaluation of your work for Chef Ayden. Don't read it. Unless you want to." She smiles at me and hands me a container of tea. "And these are tea bags I put together from my own garden. You can make tea or add it to a recipe. I'm sure you'll figure out how to use it."

I hold the bag up to my nose. Lavender, ginger, chamomile . . . "There's something in here I can't place," I say to her.

"Ah, and that's why it is magic. Not all recipes in life are easily understood or followed or deconstructed. Sometimes you have to take what is given to you and use your talents to brew the best tea possible. Yes?" She wraps me in her arms before I can answer and then she's shooing me out the door.

I take off my smock and chef's hat and fold them neatly, handing them over.

"The pork shoulder will be wonderful. I can't wait to try your marinade. Be good and safe, and oh, Emoni, trust. Okay? Trust. Yourself, mainly, but the world, too. There is magic working in your favor."

She closes the door before I can say anything else.

And for a second I feel naked, like I'm unhidden in the light of the evening sun, a person different from who I was a moment ago.

DUENDE

Pretty Leslie and I spend our last night with Mariana. She's made a big traditional meal for us and even poured us a glass of sangria. I swear to God Pretty Leslie turned Hulk-smash green at the smell of the wine and I couldn't stop the laugh that broke through my lips. She doesn't touch her glass at all.

For once, I try not to analyze the dish in front of me and just eat to enjoy. Mariana has an old-school boom box in her dining room and Spanish songs play on a loop. I recognize some from when 'Buela has her radio on in the kitchen and others I don't know but wish I did.

One song comes on and the first couple of words make me lower my fork. Mariana must notice because she gets up and turns the volume higher. Even Pretty Leslie must realize this is a beautiful song because she closes her eyes and listens.

The singer has a deep voice and the end of each note is punctuated with a clap.

"Do you recognize?" Mariana asks me. I shake my head. This is not a voice I know.

"Mercedes Sosa. Folk singer from Argentina but well-loved here."

I close my eyes. I don't want to miss another word. She sings about how everything changes, the shallow and the profound, the shiny and the old; everything but the love for home changes. I'm tapping my foot to the rhythm, and when the song ends Mariana gets up and plays the song again.

"Mercedes Sosa was full of duende. Of inspiration and passion."

I savor this new word as if it were the last bite on my plate, and I know now I'm ready to go back home.

HOME

I grab my suitcase from the conveyor belt and give Malachi a quick kiss. He pulls me back for a longer one, and I blush down to my toes as my classmates whoop and holler at seeing so much PDA. I'm almost out of the terminal when I glance behind me because I hear someone cursing up a storm. It's Pretty Leslie and her three big bags, huffing and puffing behind me toward the SEPTA sign.

"Leslie, do you need a ride? My grandmother's friend is here to pick me up. You stay over on Lehigh, right?"

Pretty Leslie doesn't need to say a word for me to see the relief written all over her face. "That would be great, Emoni. Thanks."

Mr. Jagoda is waiting right out front when we exit the terminal and he seems

445

so happy to see me. And I can't lie: it's nice to see a familiar face who's going to take me to my family. In the Volkswagen, we sit in silence listening to an oldies station. And although I fight not to run out the car every time we stop for traffic, tolls, or a red light, Mr. Jagoda's easy humming and calming demeanor helps me push back my impatience. I just want to see my baby. I couldn't even sleep on the flight or joke with Malachi because all I can think about is Babygirl. We drop Pretty Leslie off and exactly four minutes later Mr. Jagoda pulls up out front of my house.

"Will you be coming inside?" I ask Mr. Jagoda as he helps lift my bag from the trunk.

He smiles, and I love the way his eyes crinkle at the corners and his big bright teeth peek past his lips. "Oh, no. I've already seen Gloria this week and I think today she has eyes only for you." He pats my cheek and hops back into the driver's seat.

I run toward the front stairs. When I open the door, 'Buela bursts into tears from the center of the living room, where she's holding Babygirl.

Babygirl squeals and reaches for me from 'Buela's arms, and I don't even worry about the open door — I just run in and grab her to me. Inhaling her baby smell. A smell I know better than my own name. I blink up at the ceiling.

I move to 'Buela. I don't want to let go of Babygirl, so I just turn and hug 'Buela with my loose arm. She smells different, like expensive perfume, but her hands when she holds my face and kisses both cheeks still smell like vanilla.

"Pero tú sí me hiciste falta, nena." I press my cheek into her palm and nuzzle close, my eyes drifting shut.

"I missed you more, 'Buela."

ACCEPTANCE

Later that night I'm on my bed reading a magazine with Babygirl tucked into my side. Lunch with 'Buela and Babygirl was so sweet and I know all of us ate too much of 'Buela's mofongo. I only wish the jet lag hadn't hit me so hard. It wasn't until my plate of food slid off my lap that I even realized I'd been asleep. I definitely needed a little nap.

Babygirl looks twice as big as when I left her even though I know it's not possible.

"I talked with Angelica this week and she told me a lot of admission decisions went out last week. Were you able to check email in Spain?" 'Buela doesn't walk all the way into the room.

She plays with the fringes of the long gray scarf I bought her, and I notice she isn't wearing her wedding band. I want to snuggle into her familiar Spanish accent, her soft wavy hair, how firm she stands in her uniform of dress slacks and pale pullover. I don't want to tell her I was too afraid to check any of the school decisions.

"How many schools did you apply to, again?"

"Four four-year colleges and a community college," I mumble. She stands by the door, waiting. I grab my phone and log in to the first school. A rejection from Temple University. I log in to the second school. A rejection from LaSalle. I sign in to my third school. A rejection from Arcadia.

Oh shit. If I don't get in anywhere, I don't know how I'm going to tell 'Buela. There's a difference between not wanting to go to school and not even getting in.

" 'Buela, I think we should wait until tomorrow. I don't want to ruin the rest of your night."

"C'mon, nena. Just finish it. Whatever it'll be, I'd rather be with you than you find out the news alone. Faith, Emoni."

I sign into the Drexel portal.

And I slow down at what I'm seeing. 'Buela must realize my silence this time is different, because her hand stops playing with her scarf. "¿Qué fue, nena?"

I pull Babygirl into my lap and she cuddles into me without waking up. I drop a kiss on the top of her head.

I hold my phone out to 'Buela. I want her to read it herself. She closes her eyes as if saying a prayer. She scans the electronic letter and when she looks at me a big tear rolls down her cheek. She fans her face with the scarf as if it will stop the onslaught of tears, but then she's hugging me and laughing and even when Babygirl wakes up crying, all 'Buela can do is hold me on the bed and rock me, saying over and over, "Mi niña, mi niña, is going to college. Call your father. He's going to be so proud."

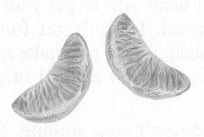

SURPRISES

I didn't think I would be accepted into Drexel. My grade point average was a little below what they say a student needs, so I'm still shocked. Unlike the guidance counselor in middle school, Ms. Fuentes pushed me to apply even though it was a reach school. It's close to home. It's a great school. And it has a culinary arts program that focuses not only on cooking, but also on restaurant management.

But I don't know how I'll help pay bills if I'm also paying for school.

" 'Buela, I need to talk to you," I say to her the next day after dinner. She mutes the TV and beams at me. Ever since my Drexel acceptance all she can do is smile at me or tear up.

"I don't want you to get your hopes up about Drexel. I didn't get full financial aid, and well, doesn't it make more sense for me to get a job instead of going into debt?"

'Buela doesn't stop smiling. She blinks as if she's waiting for the punch line of the joke but when I just repeat myself she shakes her head. "What do you mean, Emoni? This is a dream come true."

I shake my head. "I want to be in a kitchen, not in a classroom. You know I'm no good at school. What if I waste time and money and still fail my classes?"

"Emoni, you've loved your Culinary Arts class this year. I know you told me this would have more chemistry, and you're afraid of not doing well, but once you have a degree no one can take that away from you. You'll just have to work hard."

I wish I could explain that I do work hard, even in the classes I don't do well in. It's not my effort that makes learning in those classes so difficult for me. But I also know I'm not thirteen anymore. Last time I let a guidance counselor convince me I wasn't good enough to go to the school of my choice. This time around will I be the one holding myself back?

"Emoni, I've been waiting a long time for you to be able to go out into the world and fly. Do you want to know where I go when I'm pretending to be at the doctor's?"

I asked the one time and never asked again. 'Buela made it very clear it was none of my business. I don't know if I should nod or shake my head so I just stand still. Oh God. Oh God. What if 'Buela is sick? What if she just wanted me all settled because she knew something was wrong? The wall behind me is the only reason I'm standing. I brace myself for her words.

"I go to the doctor so much because sometimes I need to get away from all of . . ." She swirls her hand in the air and "all of" must mean everything in the house. "I go to the doctor to remind myself I am more than a great-grandmother to a toddler, and a grandmother to a teen mother, and a mother to a rascal of a son."

She clears her throat. "Okay. . . . The

real reason I 'go to the doctor' so much is because of Joseph, Mr. Jagoda." She doesn't look at me when she says all this and I see a blush is climbing up her brown cheek. My grandmother is blushing like a girl with her first crush. "And he's been courting me. You know he's the office manager at his son's doctor's office and he's nice to me and he took me to dinner at that fancy restaurant, and we get coffee on the weekends, and have been to a movie. He has his accent from Poland. And I have my Puerto Rican accent. We talk all the time and mostly we just sit silently. And that's probably the nicest part. I haven't sat quietly next to a man in a long time. I haven't had someone who wasn't depending on me to sew up the tears, a companion, in a long time. And nena, it's . . ." She pats her chest, and I know just what she means. "He isn't perfect! I mean, he's a Giants fan, for God's sake, but he makes me feel like a woman. Not only a mother so many times removed."

I don't know what to say to her. Her face has taken on a different look. Not so tight and pinched around the mouth; the wrinkles on her forehead have smoothed out and she drops the hand she was just swirling into the air right back onto her heart.

I sit on the couch next to her and then push my arms around her. "Oh, 'Buela. Thank goodness. I'm so glad you aren't sick or, I don't know, sitting on a park bench by yourself just to get away from us. And Mr. Jagoda? You're right, he's been so nice. I'm so glad you have someone." I squeeze her tight.

Her voice is thick when she breaks the silence. "He asked me to move in with him. He wants to marry me. And of course, I would never leave you and Babygirl. I couldn't. It wouldn't be right. Pero, Emoni, sometimes it feels nice to dream."

I don't lift my hand to wipe my cheeks. "But 'Buela, if this is what you want, don't you have to set a good example for me?"

She hiccups a laugh and pulls back from me. "I've taught you a lot, Emoni Santiago. And what I have been most proud of is what you learned about sacrifice and responsibilities. I can't shirk mine, either."

" 'Buela, I don't want you putting your life on hold for me." I remove my arms fully from around her. "That's my baby in there, you've done enough. Marry your Joe. We're going to be just fine."

JUST FINE

I don't know if we're going to be fine at all, but I try to remind myself of Mercedes Sosa's song: Everything changes. I'll learn to be fine.

Before I go to bed I call Julio. I didn't phone him once while I was in Spain and he didn't call me, either. I wish he was a texter since that would be easier, but he has conspiracy theories about the government reading people's texts.

"Emoni! Remember your viejo, finally?"

I hope he doesn't hear my sigh. "Hey, Julio. How are you?"

I hear some rustling in the background and I know I must have interrupted his reading.

"Me, I'm always the same. How was

Spain? Mami tells me you were living the good life out there in Europe."

I tell him a little bit about the trip and the apprenticeship, leaving out the Columbus monument and all the golden structures. It's too late to listen to a Julio Rant.

"Julio, I just wanted to let you know I got into college. Into Drexel here in the city. 'Buela is so excited she's probably going to start putting up posters and I wanted you to find out from me before one of your block homies called."

On the other end of the line there's silence and for a second, I think the call dropped. "Julio?"

I hear what sounds like a sniffle but that can't be true. My father didn't cry when he lost his home in the last big hurricane. Didn't cry when I stopped calling him Papi and started calling him by his first name. Doesn't cry when he visits my mother's tombstone.

But that's definitely a sniffle. "I hope Mami does put up posters. You deserve it. You must be so happy." But he must hear the hesitation in my voice because he questions, "Emoni? Is this not what you want?"

And the thing is, Julio is a lot of things. And I don't always know if I can count on him. But I do know that he believes in self-education, and if I told him I didn't want to go to school, that I thought going straight to work was a better idea, he would support me. Even if he had to argue with 'Buela to do it. But then I think about his sniffles.

"I'm happy. I'm just nervous at all the new changes."

"And Mami with her new boyfriend."

I'm stunned. 'Buela told him about Mr. Jagoda? "She told me." And I realize I asked that question out loud.

"You'll figure it out, Emoni. You've had some of the most difficult challenges thrown your way and you've always figured it out. You got angels on your shoulder."

And I can only hope he's right.

NEXT STEPS

"Ms. Santiago, how was your trip?" Ms. Fuentes asks from her desk.

I hope she doesn't look at me too closely or she'll be able to tell I was crying into my pillow all night. "It was amazing. I hope I can go back one day."

"Did you end up checking those college admissions?"

I walk to my desk and pull out a textbook immediately. I need to bury my face somewhere. "I got into Drexel."

"That's amazing, Ms. Santiago!" Ms. Fuentes claps her hands together. She drops them when I stare unenthusiastically at my closed Applied Math book. "You don't seem excited. What's wrong?"

I shake my head. "I'm fine. Still jet-lagged, I guess."

I don't look at Malachi when he walks in, but I can feel his eyes on me the entire thirty minutes of class. We spoke on the phone last night after my conversation with 'Buela. Well, mostly I spoke, which is a change for us. He listened as I listed my fears and as I cried about 'Buela. I'm so happy for her, and I'm so afraid of change.

At lunch, I can't even pretend to play with my food.

"Emoni, please explain to me why you're in crisis mode again today? You just got back from a beautiful country, you have a boyfriend, a college acceptance, and the best best friend a person could have. So what is the problem?" Angelica never has much patience with me when I'm moping.

"I feel like I'm being pulled in a hundred directions and my feet are stuck in cement."

She pushes her glasses up higher on the bridge of her nose. "So, you went to Spain and became a poet?"

I pull my hand from underneath hers

and flick applesauce at her blond curls.

"Hey!" She ducks out of the way before any lands on her and pretends to hide under the table.

"Girl, get up. I'm done reminding you who's boss here."

"Yeah, okay. Wait until I get this weave out. It's going to be straight-up apple-sauce war."

And absolutely nothing has changed. But for a few moments my chest feels lighter.

LOVE

Since I miss her so much, I pick up Baby-girl from daycare even though it's an extra half hour each way when I go there after school. Mamá Clara is super sweet and can't stop showing me Babygirl's artwork and finger paintings and all the little dresses she uses on her dolls. I haul Babygirl onto the bus and let her sing to me.

"She's such an adorable child," an older white woman says from across the aisle. "Your sister?"

I smile at Babygirl. "No, ma'am. My daughter."

The smile fades from her face but mine

stays right where it is. I've met this kind of woman before. The kind with real strict ideas about what makes certain people respectable. The kind that gets sour-faced at learning Babygirl is my daughter, but who would have sympathy if I was of a paler complexion. The kind that looks at Angelica's colorful hair and calls her ghetto under her breath, but thinks a white tween with purple corn-rows is charming and creative. She looks like the kind of woman who will break a stereotype down the middle and hold one half up for white kids and one up for black ones. And maybe I'm stereotyping her, too. Pretending to know what kind of woman she is because of the kind of women who have hated on me, and Angelica, and all the black and brown girls we know from home; who have shaken their heads and *tsk*ed their teeth, and reminded us we weren't welcome in their part of the city, on their side of the bus, in their world.

The smile stays on my face. I nuzzle Babygirl. Just the two of us. We can make it if we try.

Part Three

THE BITTERSWEET

Emoni's Recipe
"WHEN THE WORLD TRIES TO BREAK YOU, BREAK BEER BREAD WITH THOSE YOU LOVE"

Serves: Your strength when you feel alone.

Ingredients:

Three double scoops of flour
Four thumbs of white sugar
Half a stick of melted butter
Two bottles of beer
A sprinkle of sage
A sprinkle of island oregano

Directions:

1. Preheat the oven to 400 degrees. Mix all the ingredients except herbs until it's a smooth mixture. Mix sage and island oregano into

the batter.
2. Spread the mixture into a greased bread pan. Spread some more butter over the top.
3. Bake the bread for the entirety of Bad Bunny's last album.
4. Take the bread out of the oven and let cool.

*Best eaten with honey butter while listening to your own gut.

STRUCK

Over the next couple of weeks everyone keeps asking me about where I'm going to school. I usually just smile and shrug. Only 'Buela looks ready to wring my neck because she wants to write the check for the deposit, but the truth is, I know what I want to do, I just don't know how to tell anyone. Not even the people closest to me. Angelica has tried to get me to tell her about my future plans, doing everything from threatening me to mothering me to get me to talk, and today at lunch is no different.

"Emoni, you should try to eat something."

I don't look at her. She got into every school she applied to except for Pratt. They wait-listed her and she anxiously checks her email every time the security guards have their backs turned. "I'm fine. I'm not really hungry."

A shadow falls over me and I look up at smooth brown skin, bright brown eyes. Malachi. This isn't his lunch period.

"What are you doing here?" I ask him.

He straddles the cafeteria table bench and leans toward me until our foreheads touch. He doesn't smile. "You been ducking me and you won't talk to anyone and you seem sad. I figured maybe I could get an answer from you here."

I nod at him and then look down at my lunch tray.

I begin to push back from the table but then arms are around me. Malachi hugs me from behind and Angelica stands up and hugs me from the front. And I take long, deep breaths with the both of them holding me close.

Malachi tells me it's going to be okay. Angelica probably would say the same if she had a sensitive soul in her body, but she doesn't, so instead she says, "Girl, it's time to step into your own light and stop being afraid."

Both statements are helpful.

The last day before the deposit has to be postmarked, 'Buela leaves a blank check by my bedside with a note.

Follow your dreams, nena. The rest will figure itself out.

And so I complete the forms and I mail my decision.

Accepted

"I got in!" Angelica screams into the phone. "I'm coming over right now! I want you to read the email to me. I need a witness to make sure this is real!"

And I know she doesn't say Pratt Institute, but there's no other school she'd be this excited about and they were the only school to wait-list her. She must have gotten off the list. My girl is going to be heading out to New York.

I shake myself when I realize the silence has gone on a moment too long. "Angelica, I'm so excited for you! Come over. I can't wait to read the email."

I put the phone down. 'Buela is nap-ping on the couch after a big breakfast.

I close the novel I was reading for English. I don't know why I'm even doing homework anymore. The end of the year is in four weeks and teachers don't even care about schoolwork these days. It's not like they're going to fail us. A couple of them have been really "sick" lately. I've seen more subs this month than in the whole year.

There are three hard knocks on the front door and I open it without looking through the peephole.

"Angelica, 'Buela is sleeping, so —" But it's not Angelica.

It's Tyrone. Good-cologne-wearing-ass Tyrone with a puppy-dog look on his face. "Can we speak? I was hoping we could talk about something."

I step onto the stoop and pull the door closed behind me. "Tyrone, you're here" — I check my phone — "two hours early. I don't have Babygirl ready yet." Unfortunately, it's his weekend.

"I wanted to talk about that," Tyrone says. "I have an update."

"Yeah. I got an update of my own. I got into college. And I'm dating someone."

His lips tighten and he shakes his head. "Dating someone? I had heard something but I hoped it wasn't true. I don't like that."

I take a deep breath. "I know, Tyrone. I know. And for a long time, I wanted to do what everyone liked. I just need you to be there for your daughter. I'll respect you and I won't introduce her to someone unless I'm sure of who they are and that they'll be a good influence, but I'm not going to hide myself from the world. I'm not going to stop living. I'm not going to resent my kid. That's not how you care for a person."

He hasn't stopped shaking his head. "I knew you shouldn't have gone to Spain. You came back with all these crazy ideas. My mother always said you were easily influenced." I smile, because when his mother wanted to pay for my abortion, "easily influenced" was not what she'd called me.

Tyrone shoves his hands in his pockets and clears the frown off his face. I take him in. He looks more mature; his collared shirt is ironed, his hair is nicely trimmed. There's an air of confidence around him that seems less reliant on how quick he can turn a phrase and like he's actually comfortable in his own skin. I don't know when that happened but I must have missed the transformation.

"Listen, actually, that's not why I'm here. That's your business. You've taken care of Emma well so far and although I don't like it . . . I'm just not going to think about other dudes around my baby-moms and my kid.

"But I am here about Emma. I want you to know that I got a job recently, and my own apartment. So I want to help you out more with money; my mother tells me all the time babies are expensive, and I know I could be doing better by you and Emma. Even if I can't offer a lot just yet."

My heart stops for a second. Army tank Mrs. Palmer was advocating for giving me some money for Babygirl? Everything in this life really does change. But Tyrone isn't finished, and he holds up a hand as if what he has to say next isn't something

I'm going to want to hear.

"Emoni, I want to extend my visitations. Friday night to Monday morning. I think I deserve the whole weekend. Emma is always well taken care of, I pick her up and drop her off on time, and you always know how to reach me. And I'd like a full week in the summer to take her on vacation with my family."

I keep my face stone cold; I keep all my feelings tucked tight like a gymnast holds herself when she's tumbling through the air. But that's exactly how I feel, like I'm free-falling.

"Let me think about that, Tyrone. That's a big change."

"Of course. I know it's a lot to drop on you. I just, I miss her when she's not with me. Every time I see her she's grown bigger and is doing something new and . . . I don't want to miss any more moments."

I nod. "If you wait a few minutes, I'll have Babygirl ready for you. No sense in your driving back home only to turn right back around."

And I try to tell myself the same thing: forward is the only direction to go in; turning back around is for the birds.

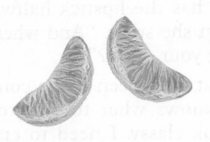

PROM

Although Malachi and I talk every day and see each other in school, we've been more chill since Spain. We've fallen into an easy rhythm of friends who kiss and talk all the time, but there's no pressure for much else.

We haven't talked about "us" and what long-distance will mean. And I'm fine with that.

"You just hanging around the house?" 'Buela says as she puts in an earring. I lean around her to watch the TV. Reruns of *Barefoot Contessa* are on.

I nod. "Yeah, just me and Babygirl."

"Is Angelica coming over?" She puts on her coat and grabs her purse.

"No. She's planning her prom outfit with Laura."

477

'Buela has the lipstick halfway to her lips when she stops. "And when are you planning your outfit?"

I nod at the screen. "The contessa just always knows what to add to make a table look classy. I need to email Aunt Sarah some of these tips."

"Emoni, you didn't hear me ask you a question. Why haven't you mentioned prom?" She sits next to me on the couch. "Nena, do you not want to go?"

"No, 'Buela, I don't. We already spent all that money for the Spain trip and my school deposit. Aren't we stretching every dollar as it is? My tips from serving lunch at school only go so far. I can't ask you to give an extra two hundred a month later."

"Apaga la televisión." And I can tell she's about to Mama Bear me, which is what she does when she wants to be strict without nagging me.

"C'mon, 'Buela. You're going to be late for your date with Joe. Can't we talk about this later?"

"A . . . pá . . . ga . . . la."

I roll my eyes and turn off the TV.

"You don't want to go to prom? Malachi didn't ask you?"

"He did. He's been asking me but he understands that it's just not something we have the money for and that I don't want to go."

"You're a woman soon. But for the next month and half, enjoy high school. Go to prom."

"The only thing I want to do on prom night is hang out here, watch JLo movies, and make delicious snacks. What do you think?"

She leans her forehead against mine. "Well, nena, I think we could live with that."

And a week later, that's exactly what I do. Malachi goes to prom but leaves early and joins us at the house. He brings me a bright-red rose, and tucks my hand into his suit pocket as we slow-dance to a corny Jennifer Lopez song. Babygirl and 'Buela clap when we are done. And it's exactly the memory I wanted.

THE RISING

I can't sleep the night before graduation. It's almost midnight. As of tomorrow afternoon, I'll be a high school graduate. And since it was my eighteenth birthday a week ago, I'm officially an adult.

Unfortunately, all I want to do is snuggle in 'Buela's lap and ask her to fix my life for me. To make the decisions. To make it all easy. Everyone's words swirl in my ear. 'Buela. Julio. Angelica. Ms. Fuentes. Aunt Sarah. Chef Amadí. Chef Ayden. Tyrone. Malachi.

Babygirl sighs in her sleep and I get up to touch her cheek. She's so peaceful and I know I'm not going to be able to sleep tonight. I tiptoe past 'Buela's bedroom and walk downstairs into the kitchen. Set the oven to 350 degrees. Grab flour. Butter. Salt. Dried oregano. A beer I planned to use to braise a steak.

Julio once told me my mom loved to bake. Aunt Sarah has confirmed it's true, although none of the recipes she's ever sent me mention them being my mother's. I mix all the ingredients together.

I'm going to have to tell 'Buela what I decided to do about college. And I'll need to make some plans for the fall. Tyrone still wants to discuss a new custody schedule, and I think I'm going to let him have more days with Babygirl. The ServSafe test results come back in a week, and I'm sure your girl did well. I've never studied harder for an exam.

The bread still has twenty minutes to go, and I'm nodding off when I hear a knock on the door. At this point it's past midnight. I grab one of the knives from the butcher block and walk quietly toward the peephole.

Standing on the front stoop is Julio. A whole month earlier than usual. I crack the door open and I think I must still be dreaming. But he sweeps me up in a hug and there's his old, familiar scent: Old

481

Spice, loc lotion, and something I've always called his "island scent."

"What are you doing here? We didn't expect you for a month," I whisper.

"What, you didn't think I would miss my only girl's graduation?"

I almost nod. I did, in fact, expect just that.

"Is everyone sleeping?" He tugs his suitcase into the living room and I close the door behind him. His bag is bigger than usual. I walk into the kitchen and he follows me, stopping at the doorway.

"Couldn't sleep, huh?" he says, rocking on his heels.

I check the oven. Still a bit more time while the top of the bread browns.

Julio and I are both standing. "You want to sit and join me, I can cut you a slice of bread in a bit."

But he's shaking his head before I even finish my sentence. "No, no, I couldn't. Did Mami cook today?"

"What, don't tell me you're gluten free," I joke. " 'Buela didn't cook today. You're stuck with my food, and I don't know if you heard, but I'm a pretty good cook."

There's a long pause. "Emoni, don't you ever wonder why whenever I visit I don't eat your cooking?"

Of course I wondered. I was just too in my feelings to ever say anything.

"Your grandmother says your food reminds her of Puerto Rico. But for me? Your food doesn't make me think of back home, it makes me think of the home I had here. Every single one of your dishes makes me think of your mother. It kills me to see memories of her face every time I take a bite of something you made. It kills me to be here in Philadelphia, and every street corner reminds me of her. I always think with time it will get easier. But it hasn't."

I'm stuck. Julio and I have never talked about my mother, and although my appetite for the bread is crushed beneath his words, my hunger to say the thing I've never said blossoms.

I walk to the sink and wash my hands. I look at my father. "I should be so angry at you. You abandoned me over and over. Why haven't I ever been enough to make you stay?"

He stuffs his hands in his pockets again. His long locs swing as he shakes his head. "It was never you, Emoni. I tried. Every year I came I said this would be the year I stayed and helped to raise my daughter. But you didn't need me. Moms did such a good job while I was gone and I wasn't built for a place like this. I miss the ocean. I miss the warmth. I miss having a real purpose. There are so many tough reminders for me here."

"But wouldn't there have been good memories, too? If you stayed long enough to make some?"

He nods. "Quizás, Emoni. Quizás. I want to keep on trying even though you are too grown to need me. I know you got a lot of changes coming, and I was thinking maybe I could stay for a while this time and help you with Emma and the bills. That could work, right? While you get used to what's coming next?"

And maybe the trying has to be enough. I take the bread out the oven and slice a piece for myself. I sit down at the table and take a bite. My father watches me closely for a moment before he reaches over and breaks off a corner. He closes his eyes. For a moment I think he'll set the bread back down. But after a long pause he pops the bread between his lips and begins chewing. I reach across the table and cover his hand.

PROMOTION CEREMONY

I have to use a whole pack of bobby pins to keep my cap sitting on my curls. We are standing outside of an auditorium at Temple University where the Schomburg graduation was held. 'Buela and Julio are snapping pictures on their phones as I hold Babygirl — she keeps running her fingers through the tassels on my cap. In my other hand I hold up my diploma. Mr. Jagoda stands in the background smiling, a calm presence, and I'm glad 'Buela invited him.

I hear someone squeal behind me and then Gelly throws an arm around my shoulders. I lean against her and smile as we pose. But her girls taking pictures without her must be too much for 'Buela to resist because she hands her phone to Mr. Jagoda and rushes to my other side.

Soon Malachi's tall figure stands next to her, tickling Babygirl. When I look up at him he blows me a kiss. Mr. Jagoda gestures someone into the picture and Ms. Fuentes winks at me, but not quick enough because I notice the tears in her eyes. Someone clears his throat, and I turn my neck to see Chef Ayden standing behind me, an arm each on Malachi and Angelica's shoulders. I have to do a double take when I see him in a sharp suit, his bald head shining in the sun. And just as we all stand straight and look at the cameras as Julio counts down, a high-pitched voice breaks in, "Can I get in, too?" Pretty Leslie doesn't wait for me to respond as she presses into Ms. Fuentes and smiles a megawatt smile.

Before Julio puts down his phone I clear my throat and ask over the sounds of all my classmates taking photos, "Mr. Jagoda, can you take a picture of the group with Julio in it, too?" Mr. Jagoda takes Julio's phone. I can tell Julio doesn't know how to feel about Mr. Jagoda yet, but he stands next to Chef Ayden behind us. 'Buela's arm comes around my waist, and it feels like it's less to support me, and more to offer comfort. To both of us.

Mr. Jagoda counts down for the last time. My family smiles for the camera.

Everyone in the picture and their families have been invited back to our house for a graduation lunch. I started cooking last night, a feast to end all feasts. I've been putting the meal together for a while now, although I didn't know exactly why I was pairing certain flavors, or how certain sides would work with one another. I was cooking toward this graduation dinner, because high school isn't the only thing I'm leaving behind.

Although my food still doesn't give me any memories, it has always been looking back; it's infused with the people I come from. But it's also a way for me to look forward: to watch the recipes that from my roots transform, grow, and feed the hungriest places inside of me.

And like a map I've been following without knowing the exact destination, I know now I've been equipping myself with tools from the journey to help me survive when I arrive. Although I don't have all the answers for what is coming next, I can finally see a glimpse of where I, Emoni Santiago, am going.

MOVING FORWARD

'Buela is at home with Julio and Babygirl. We had a big family meeting a few
days ago, and I finally laid out my plan.
'Buela won't change her mind about
what she thinks I should do. Julio hasn't
voiced an opinion outside of asking how
he can be of help. Although Babygirl
knows how to communicate exactly what
she wants, she's still not able to offer
advice outside of patting my back when I
hug her and telling me, "Good job,
Mommy."

And so, I pulled up the card Chef
Ayden's friend gave me at the Winter
Dinner. The one from the fancy restau-

rant 'Buela and I went to. I've had it on my armoire since December, with no reason to keep it, but something wouldn't let me throw it away.

I tug on my shirt before I walk into the restaurant. 'Buela ironed it for me without asking me what I needed it for. I run my palms down the front of my slacks and I'm glad that it's warm enough out that I don't need a jacket because I'm so nervous I'm sweaty, and if I was wearing layers it'd be a problem. I open the door and the hostess smiles warmly.

"Table for one?"

"No, I was . . ." I swallow hard and almost turn around. "I was hoping to speak to the chef."

"The chef? Do you mean a manager? Are you looking for a job?"

"No, I mean the chef. Is she available? She told me I could drop by."

The woman narrows her eyes as if she doesn't believe me, but she turns her perfectly bunned-up head to the side and motions to a server. She leans toward him and whispers in his ear. He nods and strides in the direction of the swinging door to the kitchen.

The hostess taps a nail on her stand. "If you'll just wait one moment."

Five minutes pass, and I know because I keep glancing at my cell phone. Six minutes. The hostess is pretending she can't see me anymore. Couples come in and glance at me to see if I'm waiting for a table, but I just keep offering them the same sickly smile and motioning them to go ahead.

Seven minutes. Eight minutes. Nine minutes. I'm about to lose my nerve and turn away when the door swings open with a bang and a woman in a high white cap and smock walks toward the hostess stand. She's as tall as I remember.

"What?" she barks at the hostess, who immediately points at me. Chef Williams turns and looks at me. Raises an eyebrow.

I straighten up. "Hello, Chef." I stick out my hand. "My name is Emoni Santiago. I'm not sure if you remember me? I was Chef Ayden's student at Schomburg Charter High School. Last winter you came to an event at my high school and you gave me your card in case I ever wanted a job."

The frown on her forehead clears up. "Yes, of course! Your food had the most amazing quality to it."

She remembers! "I came here today because I want a job. I know food better than anyone, and I was wondering if I could work for you."

She takes her hand from mine and crosses her arms and she seems to be fighting a smile. "This is a pretty demanding job, regardless of what position you start in. I don't usually hire someone so young for the kitchen staff."

"I understand. And although I'll be attending Drexel's Culinary Arts program on a part-time basis, it's not too far from here, so I can go to classes in the morning and be here by the lunchtime rush. My family is helping me out to make sure I can commit to the long hours." I give her a soft shrug. "I want to stay in Philly and work in Philly and learn from a restaurant in Philly. Because I think I have a lot to offer my hometown and the places I'm from."

She looks me slowly up and down. "How soon can you start?"

I let go of her hand and tug on the book

bag I have around my shoulders, the one that holds my chef's jacket and clogs.

"Today. Today seems like a great day to begin."

From:
ESantiago724@drexel.mail.edu
To: SarahFowlkes_15@exchange.com
Date: Thursday, August 1, 3:02 PM
Subject: re: Visit

Hi Aunt Sarah,

Thanks for my mom's pound cake recipe. I made it for my father last week and although he cried the entire time eating it, he finished every crumb. I don't know how long his visit will last, but he doesn't seem to be itching to go back just yet. He didn't renew the lease on his apartment and he's had all his barbershop tools shipped here. A cousin of his is running the barbershop in Puerto Rico. I know Philadelphia will never be able to keep him here for long, but I think he's at least planning to stay a bit longer than usual and if the pound cake helps I'll keep on making it ☺.

As to your question, Tyrone will be taking Emma on a family trip in two weeks, and I think that would be the perfect time for me to visit. I would love to come meet my cousins and my other aunts and uncles.

As to your last assignment, I did make up a recipe inspired by my name. Although Julio has told me before it means "faith," I don't think I understood why my mother might have wanted to name me that until this year. And so I decided to make a remix of flambé shrimp à la Emoni, because what better way to take a leap of faith than to set something on fire and trust it will not only come out right, but that it will be completely delicious?

I can't wait to see you in a few weeks.

With love & a sprinkling of
cinnamon, always,

E

ACKNOWLEDGMENTS

It takes a village to raise a novel, and I'm thankful for the many hands that helped push this story onward.

First and foremost, to my team at HarperTeen, I'm so lucky you all take such care of my stories; I want to give special thanks to my incredible editor, Rosemary Brosnan, and my assistant editor, Courtney Stevenson. Thanks for ushering this book through the rough, rough, *rough* stages into the story I had been trying to tell. Thanks to Erin Fitzsimmons for giving me the prettiest covers a girl could ask for. Thank you to Bess Braswell, and Ebony LaDelle and the whole Epic Reads team, who have put so much love behind this book to ensure it finds the shelves of readers.

Another special thanks to my publicist, Olivia deLeon Russo, who supports my wildest ideas for publicity and my need to bring my community to every platform.

I want to thank my agent, Ammi-Joan Paquette: I am lucky to have someone who is as fierce as she is kind guiding my way . . . and it doesn't hurt that you bake the prettiest desserts, which may or may not have inspired parts of this book!

To Carid Santos and Amanda Nazario, thanks for reading my early and ugly drafts. Your feedback is invaluable, and I know this story reads truer because of it.

To Yahaira Castro, thanks for being my critique partner. I'm so glad you ask the difficult questions that allow me to get to the heart of a book.

To Clint Smith, I appreciate you, homie! Thanks for reading this between flights and always encouraging me to center empathy.

I want to give a special thanks to Frankford High School in Philadelphia, which allowed me the privilege of teaching summer school to their seniors in 2010. Although I did not know it then, that was the first seed of this story. My heartfelt appreciation goes out to Mr. Joseph Bradbury, who in 2017 allowed me to visit his class and kitchen so I could observe his culinary arts students in action.

Hermana Jessica Tirado, you have always been a lifesaver. I'm sure only someone who has gone through the experience can fully know what it's like to be a teen mother, but I appreciate you sitting with this story and providing your thorough feedback. I hope I did it justice. And thank you for introducing me to Generation Hope. I know personally that the support they've offered so many young parents is immeasurable.

To my family, the Acevedos and the Amadis, thank you for reminding me what it means to return home. What it means to carry home with you across far-flung places. What it means to feed and love your people. What it means to come from magic. Thank you forevermore for supporting my dreams.

To my family-in-love: the Cannons, the Moyes, and the Cannon-Moyes, thank you for welcoming me to South Jersey and Ayden, North Carolina. For feeding me at Thanksgiving, for continuing our never-ending spades tournament, for sharing yourselves, and your stories, with me. And a special thanks to Nyjeri, for answering my questions about toddlers and for giving me such sweet and smart nieces; Zaria & Yara, I hope to keep trying to make the world safer and better for you, and to write stories that celebrate both your ferocity and your tenderness.

To my beloved, Shakir, here's an ode to Philly haircuts, traveling the world, and the only adage that matters: if I eat, you eat. Thanks for never letting me doubt myself, for reading everything I write, and for reminding me to celebrate even the most simple Tuesday. I love you.

Ancestors: always. Gang, gang. Who would I be if you were not? What are my stories if not but a continuation of the threads you unspooled? What do I owe you if not everything? And yet, you remind me time and again I owe you nothing but this honest, brave, full self.

Pa'lante siempre.

ABOUT THE AUTHOR

Elizabeth Acevedo is the author of *The Poet X,* which won the National Book Award for Young People's Literature, the Michael L. Printz Award, the Pura Belpré Award, and the Boston Globe-Horn Book Award. She is a National Poetry Slam champion and holds an MFA in creative writing from the University of Maryland. Acevedo lives with her partner in Washington, DC. You can find out more about her at www.acevedowrites .com.